Team Up for Success:
Building Teams
in the Workplace

Charles M. Cadwell

American Media Publishing
4900 University Avenue
West Des Moines, Iowa 50266-6769
800/262-2557

Team Up for Success:
Building Teams in the Workplace

Charles M. Cadwell
Copyright © 1997 by American Media Inc.

This publication is designed to provide accurate and authoritative information in regard to the subject matter covered. It is sold with the understanding that neither the author nor the publisher is engaged in rendering legal, accounting, or other professional service. If legal advice or other expert assistance is required, the services of a competent professional should be sought.

Credits:

American Media Publishing:	Art Bauer
	Todd McDonald
Managing Editor:	Karen Massetti Miller
Designer:	Gayle O'Brien
Cover Design:	Polly Beaver

Published by American Media Inc.
4900 University Avenue
West Des Moines, IA 50266-6769

Library of Congress Catalog Card Number 97-77104
Cadwell, Charles M.
Team Up for Success: Building Teams in the Workplace

Printed in the United States of America
1997
ISBN 1-884926-82-7

Introduction

Teams seem to be appearing everywhere in the workplace. They may not all call themselves teams; they may use terms like *task force, committee, group* or *panel.* But regardless of what they call themselves, the success of these groups depends on whether or not they learn to function as a team.

Effective teams are made up of effective members. Teams that accomplish little and have minimal impact are usually made up of individuals who either are more concerned with their own performance or who don't understand what it takes for a team to succeed.

Many teams don't rely on a single leader throughout their existence. Instead, the leadership responsibility rotates from member to member. This process ensures different perspectives and helps keep the team "fresh." It also allows team members to develop their individual leadership skills, which, in turn, makes them more effective team members.

If you are new to the team concept or part of a team that doesn't always function as well as it could, or if you want to be a more effective team member or want to learn about being a team leader, this book is for you. It addresses all these inter-related topics and provides lots of practical examples of what you can do for yourself and your team.

This book also contains numerous self-assessments and exercises that will give you the opportunity to evaluate yourself as well as your team—and more importantly, develop a plan for making any necessary improvements. Putting these skills into practice will enable you to experience the satisfaction and sense of accomplishment that comes from being a member of an effective, productive team.

About the Author

Charles M. Cadwell is the President of Training Systems +, a company based in Kansas that specializes in training system design and development. He has more than 20 years of experience in the training field.

Before starting Training Systems + in 1986, Mr. Cadwell held positions as Director of Field Training for Pizza Hut, Inc., and Director of Training for Popingo Video. He has worked with numerous Fortune 500 companies, as well as with many small and medium-sized companies.

Mr. Cadwell is the author of several books and audiocassette programs on the subjects of recruiting and selection, orientation and training, first-line supervision, coaching, empowerment, leadership, and facilitation. He also wrote *The Human Touch Performance Appraisal* and *Training That Works!* Both books were published by American Media Publishing.

Self-Assessment

This self-assessment will help you identify your team's current level of effectiveness. There is a key to help you score your answers at the end of the assessment.

	Never		Sometimes		Always	
1. Our team focuses on its mission and performance goals.	1	2	3	4	5	6
2. Team members encourage each other to achieve high levels of performance.	1	2	3	4	5	6
3. Our team resolves interpersonal conflicts.	1	2	3	4	5	6
4. Team members exhibit good interpersonal skills when working with each other.	1	2	3	4	5	6
5. Team members are committed to doing their fair share.	1	2	3	4	5	6
6. Team members avoid playing negative roles in team meetings.	1	2	3	4	5	6
7. Our team works hard to follow its charter.	1	2	3	4	5	6
8. Our team meetings are well organized and effective.	1	2	3	4	5	6
9. Team members stick to our ground rules.	1	2	3	4	5	6
10. Our team leaders are also effective team members.	1	2	3	4	5	6
11. The team members who serve as team leaders do real work.	1	2	3	4	5	6

	Never		Sometimes		Always	

12. Our team leaders keep us
    focused on results.   1   2   3   4   5   6

13. Team members are actively
    involved in team discussions.   1   2   3   4   5   6

14. Team members manage and
    resolve conflicts.   1   2   3   4   5   6

15. Our team members trust each other.   1   2   3   4   5   6

16. Our team works to achieve
    consensus more than compromise.   1   2   3   4   5   6

17. Our team uses good techniques
    to build consensus.   1   2   3   4   5   6

18. Our team takes alternative steps
    when consensus is lacking.   1   2   3   4   5   6

19. Team members understand what
    will happen when the team's goals
    are met.   1   2   3   4   5   6

20. Our team will work together to
    prepare and present a comprehensive
    final report.   1   2   3   4   5   6

21. Our team takes time to celebrate
    its accomplishments.   1   2   3   4   5   6

Use the following table to assess your ratings.

If you rated a statement 5 or 6 . . .	You have no cause for concern.
If you rated a statement 3 or 4 . . .	You sense that things aren't quite as they should be. If no changes are made, things could get worse.
If you rated a statement 1 or 2 . . .	Your team may be in serious trouble in this area. Discuss the situation with your team leader and express your concern. If you are the team leader, you and your team need to address the issue.

Write the ratings you circled next to the number of the statement. The chapters in this book that address the assessment items are listed to the right. Read the chapter to find out what you can do to help move your team in the right direction.

Statement Numbers			Chapter References
(1) _____	(2) _____	(3) _____	1: Why Teams?
(4) _____	(5) _____	(6) _____	2: Team-Member Roles and Responsibilities
(7) _____	(8) _____	(9) _____	3: Getting Organized
(10) _____	(11) _____	(12) _____	4: Becoming a Team Leader
(13) _____	(14) _____	(15) _____	5: Working Together
(16) _____	(17) _____	(18) _____	6: Team Decision Making
(19) _____	(20) _____	(21) _____	7: Wrapping It Up

● Table of Contents

Chapter *One*

Why Teams?

Chapter Objectives

▶ Define what a team is.

▶ Describe the benefits of teamwork.

▶ Explain why performance is the key to success.

▶ List four reasons why teams fail.

In order to keep ahead of its competition, Mercury Manufacturing needed to develop and introduce a new product to its distributors and retailers in six months. This was unheard of in an industry where the average time from development to market was typically 12 to 18 months. Although Mercury only had 75 employees and was considered small by industry standards, it was now facing a challenge that even industry giants had never attempted.

CEO John Bender had recently read several articles about teamwork and using teams in manufacturing. The articles made it sound easy, but John was unsure of just exactly what he needed to do. What would be considered a team at Mercury Manufacturing? What would be the real benefits of having a team? Was this the best time to give teamwork a try? Or should they wait on another project that didn't have such a critical time frame? What if the team failed?

Defining the Team Concept

A *team* has been defined as a small number of people with complementary skills who are committed to a common purpose, performance goals, and approach for which they hold themselves mutually accountable.[1] Let's break this definition down and examine its parts.

[1] Jon R. Katzenbach and Douglas K. Smith, *The Wisdom of Teams: Creating High-Performance Organizations.* New York, NY: Harper Business, 1994.

1

◆ **A small number of people**—A team may consist of as few as two people and up to as many as 25. The more people involved, the more challenging it can be to keep the team focused and get everyone involved. A team of 10 people can often accomplish more in less time than 20 people. Large teams often subdivide into smaller teams. The actual number required depends in part on the skills required.

◆ **Complementary skills**—Teams must have or develop the right mix of skills to achieve their goals. The skills needed may be technical or functional in nature, such as marketing, accounting, operations, research and development, human resources, or engineering. Problem-solving skills are also critical when the team must make decisions or deal with logjams. Interpersonal skills take on greater significance as members spend more and more time together. Members have to be able to get along with each other and put team results ahead of individual accomplishment.

◆ **Purpose and goals**—Teams must have a reason for being. The purpose must be clear to all members. The broad purpose must then be further defined with goals that are as specific as possible so team members understand what is expected. Goal setting can be done by the team itself as it is getting organized to accomplish its broad purpose. The purpose should be something that excites and challenges team members. For most people, being on a team to decide where to put the microwave oven in the break room would not be as exciting as helping develop a new product.

A team's purpose must be clear to all members.

◆ **Common approach**—Teams need to agree on how they will work together to achieve their objectives. A set of ground rules and expectations must be clear to all members. A few of the questions that must be answered are:

• What are the responsibilities of team members?

• What roles are members expected to play?

• What format will be used for making decisions?

• How will meetings be structured?

◆ **Mutually accountable**—Successful teams understand that they are in this together. It doesn't matter what each individual thinks or does unless it contributes to the team's success. Team members must keep their commitments to each other. There must also be consequences for not meeting commitments or not supporting the work of other team members. A well-defined, challenging purpose can excite members and help foster a sense of mutual accountability.

Take a Moment
Are You Part of a Team?
How well does your work group measure up to being a team? Check those parts of the definition that apply. For those that you can't check, briefly describe what needs to be changed so you will be a team.

❑ We have from 2 to 25 members.
Corrective steps are:

_____

_____

❑ Members have complementary skills.
Corrective steps are:

_____

_____

❑ We have a clear purpose and specific goals.
Corrective steps are:

_____

_____

Continued on next page

Take a Moment *(continued)*

❏ We have a common approach.
Corrective steps are:

_____

_____

❏ We hold each other accountable.
Corrective steps are:

_____

_____

Reaping the Benefits of Teamwork

From Fortune 500 companies to small nonprofit organizations, teams are becoming more and more common in the workplace. Manufacturing firms, service organizations, new business start-ups, churches, retail stores, civic organizations, and governmental agencies have formed teams to get more done. Why? Organizations that have switched to a team approach have found that teams offer several benefits:

◆ Teams accomplish more with less waste. They make the best use of their resources and are more productive than their counterparts who don't have as clear a sense of direction.

◆ Team members produce higher-quality work. They know that several other people will be looking at their results, and they want to do a good job.

◆ Team members are happier. People who feel they are making a contribution enjoy what they are doing and are often willing to do even more.

◆ Team members have the opportunity for personal development. People in teams are often "stretched" to develop new skills in order to help the team meet its goals. They are also exposed to new and different ways of doing things.

Teams accomplish more with less waste.

◆ Teams are more flexible in how they approach problems. In turn, this gives organizations more flexibility in how they deploy their people.

◆ Customer satisfaction is higher. Teams can produce higher quality and focus on meeting customer needs better than one person can.

Take a Moment

Is Your Organization Reaping the Benefits of Teamwork?

Check the benefits your organization is getting from teams.

❏ People are more productive.
❏ People produce higher-quality work.
❏ People are happier.
❏ People are getting personal development.
❏ People are more flexible.
❏ Customer satisfaction is higher.

What needs to be done to take advantage of these benefits?

_____

_____

_____

Performance: The Key Driver of Team Success

The most successful teams are those that focus on performance.

The most successful teams are those that focus on performance. Successful athletic teams focus on giving the best performance possible day in and day out. The result is that together they win more often than they lose. In the workplace, the most respected teams are those whose performance clearly makes a significant contribution to the organization's success. Others in the organization easily recognize their accomplishments. Most people want to be a part of, and associated with, successful teams—teams that perform. It only makes sense that if organizations want to be successful, they need to develop performance-oriented teams. Let's look at how teams and performance go together.

◆ **Performance is the goal, not having a team.**
If everyone could achieve more by working individually, there would be no need for teams. In most cases, the combined efforts of 10 committed individuals directed toward a specific goal will create synergy and result in better performance than the sum of 10 individual efforts. When an organization truly wants to improve performance, it should consider forming a team to take advantage of the benefits.

◆ **Performance challenges energize team members.**
When faced with a seemingly insurmountable goal or obstacle, teams rise to the occasion. Individual members increase their commitment because each one wants the team to succeed. The rush of adrenaline that one person experiences energizes other team members. Team success increases members' enthusiasm and energy, so they put forth more effort and become even more successful. The cycle repeats itself as success and enthusiasm continually build until the team achieves optimal performance.

◆ **Performance should focus on results that balance the needs of customers, employees, and stakeholders.**
Exceptional performance takes into consideration the needs of all who will be affected by the results. Whatever the team accomplishes for the organization, it has to consider what the impact will be on three constituent groups: customers, employees, and stakeholders. While the results will not always be equally balanced for all three groups, there must be a sense of proportion.

> ■ A team recommends that customers be given a huge price break, which results in happy customers. As a result of the team's action, however, the company's profitability suffers, and eventually some employees have to be laid off. The loss of profits also causes stakeholders to experience a decline in the value of their stock. A decision that looked good for one constituent group turned out to be bad for the other two. Effective teams consider the impact their performance-related decisions will have on all three groups before deciding on the best course of action.

> In most cases, the combined efforts of 10 committed individuals directed toward a specific goal will create synergy and result in better performance than the sum of 10 individual efforts.

**Team
performance
can be
bolstered
by strong
individual
performance.**

◆ **Performance challenges encourage high levels of individual performance, which contributes to team success.**
It has been said that a chain is only as strong as its weakest link. Teams are much the same. However, team performance can be bolstered by strong individual performance. Successful teams almost always include one or more individuals who contribute at a high level but still recognize the importance of all team members. The basketball player who scores 40 points in a winning cause recognizes that the players who rebounded and passed her the ball also played an important role in helping the team win. A weak team, on the other hand, is one where many members give less than their best and expect someone else to pick up the slack—a series of weak links that makes for a weak team. Great teams are made up of many people who are committed to doing their individual best because they know it will contribute to the team's success.

◆ **Performance challenges encourage team discipline and organization.**
Teams must have discipline to succeed, and they must be organized. Effective teams are made up of people who understand that the team's success depends on each person having the necessary discipline to persevere and work to ensure that the team achieves its common purpose. All team members must know where they fit in and how what they do is related to the responsibilities of other team members. Well-organized teams consist of individuals who are all headed in the same direction—toward the team's common purpose.

Take a Moment

Is Performance Driving Your Team?

Your answers to the following questions will help you evaluate what is driving your team.

1. What are your team's performance goals (its common purpose)?

   _____

   _____

2. How are you giving consideration to the needs of customers, employees, and stakeholders?

   _____

   _____

3. List some examples of high levels of individual performance that have contributed to team success.

   _____

   _____

4. How would you rate the discipline of team members? High, low, or somewhere in between? Why?

   _____

   _____

5. How would you rate the organization of team members? High, low, or somewhere in between? Why?

   _____

   _____

Why Teams Fail

Being on a team doesn't guarantee success. Some so-called teams fail and are disbanded without ever achieving any significant degree of success. Other teams seem to achieve success beyond what anyone thought possible when they were formed. What is the difference between success and failure? Let's examine four reasons why teams fail.

◆ **The team lacks a shared purpose or focus.**
This goes right back to the heart of our definition of a team. Teams are "committed to a common purpose." While there may be individual successes, the team as a whole can't succeed until everyone is headed in the same direction.

◆ **Team members are not committed.**
Some people agree to be on teams just to get out of a current situation; they have no strong ties to the other team members or the team's goal. Some members may be more interested in getting personal recognition for their work. Others simply don't have the internal motivation to be as disciplined and organized as necessary to contribute to team success.

◆ **The team lacks support and/or resources.**
Teams can fail when they don't have the necessary support or resources to accomplish their goals. Some examples include:

> **Teams can fail when they don't have the necessary support or resources to accomplish their goals.**

■ A team is formed to solve an ongoing scheduling problem, but management ignores the team's recommendations.

■ A team is formed to test several different distribution methods, but management doesn't provide the team with a budget to do so.

■ A team has a task that requires seven people, but management assigns only three people to the project.

In each case, the lack of support and/or resources can prevent an enthusiastic group from ever becoming a team, and it can put a damper on the most enthusiastic team members.

◆ **Team members fail to resolve interpersonal conflicts.**
Teams will fail when members are working at cross-purposes
or are unable to get along with each other. One person may
think another person is trying to be too assertive. People
may be less than honest in dealing with each other. Some
people seem to thrive on conflict and don't think it affects
performance. Some conflict can be positive if it challenges
members to improve performance. Negative conflict that is
allowed to go unchecked, on the other hand, can keep the
team from accomplishing its objectives.

Take a Moment
Is Your Team Headed for Failure?
Check the reasons that apply to your team. For those that
you check, briefly describe what needs to be done so your
team won't fail.

❏ We lack a shared purpose or focus.
  Corrective steps are:

  _____

  _____

❏ Team members are not committed.
  Corrective steps are:

  _____

  _____

❏ There is a lack of management support and/or
  resources.
  Corrective steps are:

  _____

  _____

Continued on next page

Take a Moment *(continued)*

❑ Interpersonal conflicts are not being resolved.
Corrective steps are:

_____

_____

There may be other reasons why your team seems headed for failure. List those here and what corrective steps you think need to be taken.

❑ _____

Corrective steps are:

_____

_____

❑ _____

Corrective steps are:

_____

_____

Teams Don't Last Forever

Team members should be made aware that there will be a time to dissolve the team.

Teams are usually formed to work on specific projects or to address unique problems. Team members may come from different parts of an organization and work together for a specific period of time. Team members should be made aware that there will be a time to dissolve the team and that they will have to move on to other tasks or back to their original assignments. Teams members must be willing to accept this fact of team life. Some specific guidelines for when and how to disband a team are covered in Chapter 7.

1

Take a Moment

Think about all the kinds of teams with which you have been involved but that are no longer active. Check those that apply:

- ❏ Sports teams
- ❏ Fundraising groups
- ❏ Musical groups
- ❏ Church committees
- ❏ Project teams
- ❏ Civic organizations
- ❏ Boy Scouts or Girl Scouts
- ❏ School committees
- ❏ Volunteer organizations
- ❏ Cast member for a play
- ❏ Debate team
- ❏ Cheerleader
- ❏ Other _____
- ❏ Other _____

Chapter Summary

More and more organizations are benefiting from using teams. The most successful teams are the ones that focus on performance. Teams that don't focus on performance, have members who are not committed, lack support and/or resources, or have interpersonal conflicts often fail.

Self-Check: Chapter 1 Review

Complete each of the following statements. Suggested answers are on page 114.

1. A team is a small _____ of people with

   _____ skills who are committed to a

   common _____, _____

   goals, and approach for which they hold themselves

   _____.

2. List three benefits of teamwork to team members.

   a. _____

   b. _____

   c. _____

3. The key driver of successful teams is _____.

4. Team performance should focus on results that balance the

   needs of _____, _____,

   and _____.

5. List two reasons why teams sometimes fail.

   a. _____

   b. _____

Chapter *Two*

Team-Member Roles and Responsibilities

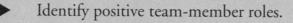

Chapter Objectives

▶ List the qualities of effective team members.

▶ Identify positive team-member roles.

▶ Identify negative team-member roles and strategies for dealing with them.

Mike caught the bat in his left hand midway between the two ends. Julie quickly put her hand above his, and Mike countered by placing his right hand above hers. A split second later, Julie put her other hand on the bat. The exchange continued, hand over hand, until Julie's hand was at the end of the bat. Mike used his fingers to clutch the knob and declared, "I get first choice."

Many of us have been in Mike's or Julie's shoes. Others of us have watched this scene played out many times and wondered if we would be picked first or last or somewhere in between. The Mikes and Julies of the world have had a lot of experience in choosing team members. But choosing a pitcher in the fourth grade and selecting a team member for a major organization project is not exactly the same thing. Or is it?

Identifying the Qualities of Effective Team Members

An effective team requires effective team members. There are four qualities that are necessary to contribute to a team and to ensure an atmosphere of teamwork. These are qualities the person may already possess or qualities the person has the potential to develop while working with the team. As

> An effective team requires effective team members.

mentioned earlier, being part of team can be a developmental opportunity for some people. However, you wouldn't want every team member to be selected for development purposes. In order for the team to be effective, some team members should already possess the four key qualities described below.

◆ **Expertise**
Team members should be acquainted with the situation or problem they will be assigned. The more knowledge and expertise team members can bring to the table, the better. Otherwise, some valuable team time will need to be spent bringing members up to speed.

■ **Example:** When the CEO at Mercury Manufacturing forms a team to develop and introduce a new product, team members should have some expertise in the requirements of that task. Their previous experience could help the team avoid wasting time and money.

◆ **Impact**
People create impact by the quality of their contributions to the team. Members with impact are also able to convince or influence others (in a positive manner) when necessary so the team keeps moving forward.

Teams themselves have an impact on groups both inside and outside the organization. Teams should try to choose members who can represent groups affected by what the team does.

■ **Example:** As Mercury Manufacturing forms its new product development team, the organization should draw on members who understand the impact their actions could have on customers, employees, or stakeholders.

◆ **Commitment**
Team members must be willing to put forth the time and effort required to accomplish the team's task. Without commitment, team members are more likely to take short-cuts or circumvent the team's common purpose.

People who are committed to the team will continue to work during difficult as well as easy situations. While they might become discouraged, they are committed to "sticking to it"

Without commitment, team members are more likely to take short-cuts or circumvent the team's common purpose.

25

until the job is done. Their commitment is also reflected in their willingness to do their fair share of the work to make the team successful.

◆ **Interpersonal skills**

A person's ability to get along with and work with others can be the "make or break" quality of an effective team member. A person who has great expertise, impact, and commitment but can't get along with others can bog down the entire team. Those who have difficulty controlling their egos do not make good team members. They are more likely to be concerned about the impression they make than with the team's results. A key part of our definition of a team is "they hold themselves mutually accountable." Holding another person accountable when there is no direct reporting relationship requires good interpersonal skills.

> A person's ability to get along with and work with others can be the "make or break" quality of an effective team member.

Take a Moment

Can you be an effective team member? Think about a team you are currently on or one that you might be joining. Do you have, or can you develop, the following qualities:

1. Expertise
   - I am knowledgeable about the project.   Yes   No
   - I have relevant experience.   Yes   No
   - I offer a unique perspective on the situation.   Yes   No

2. Impact
   - I can clearly communicate my ideas.   Yes   No
   - I can influence others in a positive manner.   Yes   No
   - I understand the impact of the team's possible decisions.   Yes   No

3. Commitment
   - I have the time to devote to the team.   Yes   No
   - I am willing to do whatever is needed.   Yes   No
   - I am the type who "sticks to it."   Yes   No

Continued on next page

Take a Moment *(continued)*

4. Interpersonal Skills

• I like working with other people.	Yes	No
• I get along with other people.	Yes	No
• I can work out interpersonal problems.	Yes	No
• I want others to hold me accountable.	Yes	No

Total: Yes _____ No _____

The Yes responses indicate your ability to be an effective team member. If you marked No to any items, you will need to work on making some improvements in these areas.

Mastering Team-Member Roles

Consciously or unconsciously, most team members will assume roles that affect the way they contribute. Some roles can be viewed as positive, because they help the team move forward, while others tend to be negative, because they hamper the team's progress.

> **Most team members will assume roles that affect the way they contribute.**

The roles described here are not roles that are assigned. Rather, they are the roles that some people tend to naturally take anytime they are part of a team. (In later chapters, we will consider more formal team roles that can be assigned.) Let's begin by examining the positive roles.

Positive Team-Member Roles

◆ Facilitator
This person sees his or her role as keeping the team on track. The facilitator may also be the team leader. In some cases, however, the facilitator acts as more of an assistant to the team leader to make sure the group doesn't get bogged down. In either case, you can recognize the facilitator by these types of behaviors:

• Takes control of the situation to keep things on track.

• Expresses concern for the team's goals and objectives.

- Sees things from the organization's point of view.

The following example illustrates a facilitator at work.

Carl:
That's an interesting point, Joan. Would it be okay if we table it for a moment, though, since it's not directly related to the subject at hand?

Joan:
As long as we don't forget it altogether.

Carl:
I'll make sure of that. As a matter of fact, I think we'll need to discuss that in some detail when we get to the next phase of our assignment.

Carl has assumed the role of facilitator to make sure that the team keeps on track and moving toward its common purpose.

◆ Troubleshooter
This person is always on the lookout for problems that may arise as the team goes about its work. A good troubleshooter goes beyond just pointing out problems. She or he also recommends or gets the team to identify alternatives that will solve the problem. Troubleshooters also look ahead and see potential problems that may occur in the future as the result of actions being taken at the moment. Like the facilitator, the troubleshooter is concerned about the team's goals and objectives.

> The trouble-shooter is always on the lookout for problems that may arise as the team goes about its work.

◆ Investigator
Every team needs a person who knows where to go for the most current information on a subject. Like Sherlock Holmes, the investigator knows what questions to ask and can interpret the answers. Investigators on your team will say things like:

- "I know someone who can help us."

- "I've recently read an article about that."

- "I know where there's some extra money in the budget."

A good investigator can be extremely beneficial in gathering information the team can use when making decisions. Since the investigator enjoys the role, he or she does not see the extra work as negative, but rather as a way to contribute to the team.

◆ **Smoother**
When conflicts arise, the smoother springs into action. The smoother helps defuse difficult situations and encourages people to focus on issues, not personalities. The smoother also makes sure people keep an open mind and listen to each other's points of view, as in this example:

2

> The smoother helps defuse difficult situations and encourages people to focus on issues, not personalities.

Sally:
There's no need to argue about that. You both have good points.

Bill:
But I think Joe is trying to make things more difficult than necessary.

Joe:
Not at all. You just aren't listening.

Sally:
Why don't you explain your idea some more, Joe? Then Bill can ask any questions he has.

Having a smoother can be extremely beneficial when a team is dealing with issues that get people stirred up or even angry with each other. The smoother knows how to find ways around difficult situations.

◆ **Encourager**
A good encourager will help keep all members involved in what the team is doing and let them know that their contributions are important and needed. If some members seem reluctant to participate, the encourager may call on them and ask them what they think about a particular issue. The encourager helps build confidence by providing positive feedback to team members for their contributions. An encourager will also volunteer to help another team member with an assignment or ask a team member to use his or her skills and take on a certain assignment.

The challenger
keeps
everyone
honest and
helps clarify
key points.

◆ Challenger

The challenger keeps everyone honest and helps clarify key points. Sometimes seen as abrasive or combative, a positive challenger really just wants to make sure that all members are saying what they think and that they mean what they say, as in the following example:

Tom:
I think we should just throw out what we've been doing in the past and start using the new system immediately.

Roberta:
Do you really believe that, Tom?

Tom:
(Pause) I have tried parts of the system and had some success. Some of it didn't work so well, though.

Roberta:
How about telling us exactly what succeeded and what failed?

Roberta's challenge to Tom will ensure that the team has a clearer understanding of Tom's prior experience. Without her challenge, team members may have accepted Tom's original comment at face value. Worse yet, they may have made a decision based on incorrect or insufficient reasoning. The best challengers know that they must challenge ideas, but not personalities.

These positive roles, when assumed by various team members, can help keep a team moving toward its objectives. As mentioned earlier, these roles usually do not need to be assigned, but will occur naturally on most teams. However, if the roles seem to be missing from your team, you may need to become an encourager and explain how different people could assume these roles to help the team in a positive manner.

Negative Team-Member Roles

On the flip side of the team experience are the negative team member roles. These negative roles can cause problems for all team members. If allowed to go unchecked, they can become a distraction and impede the team and its work. The chart that follows describes some typical negative behaviors, the possible reason for each behavior, and strategies for dealing with the behavior.

2

Behavior	Reason for behavior	Strategies
Dominator	Likes to be the center of attention.	Call on other team members by name.
	Wants to show expertise.	Interrupt politely and indicate you want others' input.
	Wants to make sure his or her ideas are heard first.	Avoid eye contact.
Nonparticipator	Bored or indifferent.	Privately determine the reason for not participating.
	Doesn't want to be part of team.	If superior, ask for comments based on experience.
	Feels superior to others Shy and/or insecure.	If shy or insecure, ask questions to draw out; compliment ideas.
Arguer	Likes to argue (sometimes even when he or she agrees).	Be alert to honest critical thinking.
	Does not agree with other participants.	Control your tendency to get into a debate.
	Prefers debate to resolving issues.	Refer comments to the team and let them make the point.

Behavior	Reason for behavior	Strategies
Inquisitor	Tries to put people on the spot.	Never take sides.
	Wants to hear others' views before giving her or his own.	Explain that the team's ideas are most important.
	May be sincerely interested in other viewpoints.	Reserve your opinion until the team has expressed its ideas.
Naysayer	Never satisfied.	Suggest a private meeting to discuss the concern.
	Likes to create negative atmosphere.	Have team members respond with positives.
	Always sees the negative ("It won't work").	Stress benefits of being positive.
	May have a legitimate complaint.	Be willing to listen to legitimate concerns.

Some of these negative behaviors are more likely to appear early as the team is developing and members are getting to know each other. Over time, these behaviors may fade away and no longer be a problem. It's important to look for patterns of behavior and not to be overly concerned with infrequent displays of negative behavior.

Take a Moment

What role will you play on your team? Read each pair of statements below and mark the one that most accurately describes the role you are likely to assume.

2

_____ I have many of things to tell team members. (b)
_____ I can learn from what others have to say. (a)

_____ I know who to talk to and where to go to get information. (a)
_____ I prefer to discuss and/or challenge the current information rather than bring in more data. (b)

_____ I am concerned about meeting team goals and objectives. (a)
_____ I want to make sure my ideas are heard, regardless of the team's final decision. (b)

_____ I think the more disagreement the better. (b)
_____ I like to keep people honest without making them feel uncomfortable. (a)

_____ I prefer to get all the ideas out on the table. (a)
_____ I usually have better ideas than most people. (b)

_____ I like to foresee problems and prevent them. (a)
_____ I think most problems will go away if ignored. (b)

Totals: (a) _____   (b) _____

The (a) items represent the more positive team roles while the (b) items represent the more negative team roles. Review any of your (b) responses and indicate below any changes you think you need to make.

_____

_____

_____

_____

Chapter Summary

Effective teams have members who either possess—or have the ability to develop—expertise, impact, commitment, and interpersonal skills. Once on board the team, some members will play positive roles that move the team forward. Others may assume negative roles, which must be dealt with if the team is to be successful.

Self-Check: Chapter 2 Review

Complete each of the following statements. Suggested answers are on pages 114 and 115.

1. List four qualities of effective team members.

    a. _____

    b. _____

    c. _____

    d. _____

2. Team members who do not possess the necessary qualities must have the _____ to develop the qualities.

3. The "make or break" quality needed by all team members is effective _____.

4. Match the following Positive Team Roles and their descriptions.

    _____ Facilitator   a. Recommends alternatives.
    _____ Troubleshooter   b. Makes sure everyone
                                  contributes.
    _____ Investigator   c. Takes control of the
                                  situation.
    _____ Smoother   d. Helps resolve conflicts.
    _____ Encourager   e. Knows who to talk to.

5. Match the following Negative Team Roles and the strategy for dealing with them.

    _____ Dominator   a. Discuss concerns in
                                  private.

    _____ Arguer   b. Explain the importance
                                  of team ideas.

    _____ Nonparticipator   c. Avoid getting into a
                                  debate.

    _____ Inquisitor   d. Avoid eye contact.

    _____ Naysayer   e. Ask questions to get
                                  involved.

2

Chapter *Three*

Getting Organized

Chapter Objectives

▶ Develop a team charter.

▶ Lead and/or participate in team meetings.

▶ Establish team ground rules.

"It looks like everyone is here now, so let's get started," Michelle said.

"What time were we supposed to start?" asked Mike.

"I thought it was 15 minutes ago," chimed in Jack.

"Where did you get your information? Michelle told me we would start between 8:00 and 8:15," said Mary.

"I was hoping everyone would be here at 8:00, but I figured realistically we'd be lucky to get started by 8:15," explained Michelle.

"Then why didn't you just say 8:15?" asked Mike. "I could have finished checking my voice mail."

"As if someone would leave you a message," chided Jack.

Wise team leaders ask the members for help in identifying the kinds of rules that make sense for the team.

It's Michelle's turn to lead the team meeting, but it seems to be off to a somewhat rocky start. That could be because her team hasn't yet established its charter, meeting guidelines, or team ground rules. Whether you are a team leader or a team member, you should be involved in developing these guidelines for your team. Wise team leaders ask the members for help in identifying rules that make sense for the team. They also work with the team to develop and document the rules *before* they are needed. This preplanning is important, because in many teams the leadership role is rotated among team members. Regardless of your role, you will be able to make positive contributions if you understand how to lay the groundwork for your team's success.

Writing a Team Charter

An effective team takes time to decide how it will work to achieve its objectives. It does so by writing a team charter. The team's charter establishes its purpose and goals, identifies any constraints or parameters, and explains how the team will function. A well-developed team charter makes it easy for all team members to understand what is expected of them and helps keep them focused on their common purpose. A team charter is a proactive document that seeks to lay the groundwork for dealing with issues and situations that may arise in the future. The team charter should include each of the following seven items.

Item 1: Mission or Performance Goals

Teams need to have a sense of common purpose so that all team members are committed to the same goal. Some teams establish a formal mission statement, while others establish a set of specific performance objectives. The approach chosen will depend on the team and what works best for its members. The process of defining the team's mission can help team members develop a sense of direction and camaraderie. As they work together to define their purpose, team members will get to know each other and begin to develop common bonds and a commitment to being a part of the team.

In many cases, the team's mission or performance goals will be influenced by management. If management decided to form the team in the first place, it had some reason in mind. The team must consider any management input it receives. However, the team may go beyond management's expectations as it defines its mission.

■ **Example:** An organization may form a team to review the way the organization provides training. The team may start with a review of training as its basic premise, but it may find that it also has to consider how other factors, such as hiring decisions and the work environment, affect training. If the team decides to expand its purpose beyond its original charge from management, it must go back to management to verify that this change is acceptable.

3

> The team's charter establishes its purpose and goals, identifies any constraints or parameters, and explains how the team will function.

37

Once agreement
is reached on
the mission or
performance
goals, the team
must define
what it will
produce.

Item 2: Deliverables

Once agreement is reached on the mission or performance goals, the team must define what it will produce. Again, management most likely will have some input into this discussion. The easiest way to think of deliverables is to answer this question: "What will be the end result of our efforts?" Answering that question will lead to several others:

◆ Does the team prepare a written report? If so, is it a statement of the current situation only, or does it include recommendations as well?

◆ What action, if any, is the team authorized to take?

◆ To whom will the team report its results?

◆ Will there be a formal presentation of results?

◆ How much time does the team have to complete its assignment?

Item 3: Budget

The question of finances must also be addressed as the team develops its charter. Some of the budget questions that need to be answered include:

◆ How much money is budgeted for the team?

◆ Does the team have its own budget, or does it share part of someone else's budget?

◆ Does anyone have to approve expenditures?

◆ Are budget reports to be submitted?

◆ Who is in charge of tracking the team's budget?

◆ What if the team needs additional funding?

Knowing the answers up front will enable the team to make informed decisions as it plans its strategy and begins its work.

Item 4: Team Name

A team name provides a sense of identity. How would fans react if the New York Yankees were just called New York? Or if the Chicago Bulls were just called Chicago? Most likely, fans wouldn't have the same level of enthusiasm they demonstrate by purchasing, wearing, or displaying items with the team name.

Your team's name doesn't have to be creative or linked to a symbol such as bombers, hawks, or heat. Often, a workplace team will take its name from what it was organized to do. Some typical examples include Training Team, Design Group, Distribution Task Force, or Implementation Team. At the same time, don't overlook the value of a unique name. For example, Kodak has its Zebra Team, which is responsible for producing the company's black-and-white film products.

3

Item 5: Team Members and Their Roles

In Chapter 2, we discussed the qualities of effective team members and some of the roles that team members consciously or unconsciously play. There are also other, more formal roles that the team may assign to specific members. The team charter should specify who the members of the team are and what functional roles they will play. Some formal team roles include:

- Team leader—provides direction and focus.

- Secretary—takes and distributes minutes of meetings.

- Treasurer—keeps track of budgets and spending.

- Coordinator/Administrator—some teams designate a person to contact team members for special meetings, to interface with other departments, and to handle various administrative duties that may be required.

The team charter should specify who the members of the team are and what functional roles they will play.

The number and type of assigned roles will vary depending on the number of people on the team and how the team will function. Some teams rotate formal roles among their members so that everyone gets the opportunity to be the leader. Roles may be assigned by management, members may volunteer for specific roles, or team members may elect each other to specific jobs. Regardless of the method, the important thing is to assign formal roles early in the process to prevent such later comments as "I didn't know I was supposed to do that," or "Someone should have taken care of that."

39

Item 6: Authority Level

A team needs to know how much authority it has to take action. Some teams are formed solely for the purpose of doing research and making recommendations. An example of this type of team is a group of employees who are asked to research various models of microwave ovens that cost $500 or less and to make a recommendation on which one to purchase for the employee break room. But the authority of other teams is less clear-cut, as in the following example.

■ Management has formed a team to design a new computer system. The team is expected to contact several companies, evaluate numerous pieces of hardware and software, field-test one or more systems, analyze results, and make recommendations. How much authority does this team have? Does it need to have any of its decisions reviewed, or does it have free reign to do whatever it thinks is necessary? Are there budgetary constraints? How much interaction can it have with other departments? What if it needs additional human resources?

Defining a team's authority level in the beginning can reduce headaches in the future.

Defining a team's authority level in the beginning can reduce headaches in the future.

Item 7: Reporting Relationships and Reports

Teams don't operate in a vacuum. They are normally formed from members of a larger organization. They don't decide to form on their own—usually, someone or some group decides that a team is needed. Once the team is formed, questions about reporting relationships and written reports need to be answered:

◆ To whom does the team report?

◆ Are progress reports required? If so, how often and to whom?

◆ How much, if any, ongoing involvement will there be by management or others outside the team?

◆ Will the team receive feedback about its work?

Answers to these questions will help the team as it makes decisions about how to organize to accomplish its mission.

Take a Moment

Consider a team of which you are a member or a team you have been asked to lead. Fill in the basics of your team's charter.

Our mission (performance goals) is/are:

_____

_____

Deliverables are:

_____

_____

Our budget is:

_____

Our team name is:

_____

Team Members   Team Roles

_____   _____

_____   _____

_____   _____

Our authority level is:

_____

Our reporting relationship is:

_____

Required Reports   When Due

_____   _____

_____   _____

_____   _____

3

41

Conducting Team Meetings

Effective team meetings serve several purposes. Some of the more common ones are:

◆ To provide an opportunity for team members to connect with one another.

◆ To review progress that has been made since the last meeting.

◆ To discuss problems that have been encountered.

◆ To plan for the future.

In most teams, the designated leader conducts the meetings. In some teams, however, the leadership of the meeting rotates from one team member to another. Chances are, if you are part of a team, you will be asked to lead a meeting at some point. This section will help you prepare to lead a meeting when it's your turn. And, even if you aren't the leader, knowing about some meeting basics can help you be a more effective participant.

Preparing an Agenda

A well-planned and well-run meeting starts with an agenda.

Meetings without agendas tend to be unfocused, which wastes time. A well-planned and well-run meeting starts with an agenda. The agenda doesn't need to be fancy or complex—in fact, the simpler, the better. The agenda is simply an outline to guide the leader and participants and keep them on track.

In most cases, the same basic agenda can be used for all team meetings (see the Typical Team Meeting Agenda on the next page). This saves team members the work of preparing a new agenda every time and provides continuity from one meeting to the next. But just because the meeting follows the same order every time doesn't mean you can forego a written agenda. All team members should have an agenda in front of them when the meeting starts.

Typical Team Meeting Agenda

1. **Review of team mission or performance goals**
   It's always good to remind members why the team was formed. Often team members get so wrapped up in their daily activities that they lose sight of what they are supposed to be doing. Some creative team leaders put the team mission at the top of the agenda so it's the first thing everyone sees.

2. **Announcements**
   Time should be set aside for sharing information for administrative purposes. Team meetings can be a good time to "pass the word" about something to everyone at once. Having announcements up front also lets members know of things that could affect their work plans. For example, an announcement that the computer system will be down for a couple of hours the next morning would help members as they plan their next day's activities.

3. **Progress reports from team members**
   This is a crucial part of the meeting as team members share with each other what they have accomplished since the last meeting. Unfortunately, progress reports can also be time-consuming and boring if members go into too much detail and provide irrelevant information. Here's what you can do to avoid these problems:

   ◆ First, establish a time limit for reports—and stick to it.

   ◆ Second, have other participants hold their questions and comments until the end of the report.

   ◆ Third, have a predetermined outline for the progress reports. For example, a typical progress report might include:

     • Objective

     • Current status

     • What was accomplished

     • Any needed assistance or resources

     • Next steps

Establish a time limit for reports—and stick to it.

43

Dwelling on problems without generating solutions not only wastes time but also can destroy morale.

4. **Issues, problems, and solutions**

   One of the benefits of having a team is being able to involve others in helping team members who are having problems. Make sure these sessions stay productive by focusing on solutions rather than complaints. Dwelling on problems without generating solutions not only wastes time but also can destroy morale.

5. **Planning for the future**

   Set aside time for identifying what will happen next. Review any assignments or commitments made during the meeting as well as specific deadlines for accomplishing the task. Often, a To-Do list can be developed throughout the meeting, and then the list can be used as a summary of the team's plan. The last thing to do is set the next team meeting date while all participants are still present. If you wait until after the meeting to set the next one, you'll wind up pulling your hair out trying to coordinate everyone's schedules.

Take a Moment

Use the guidelines just suggested as well as your experience and knowledge to develop an agenda for your next team meeting.

_____

_____

_____

_____

_____

_____

_____

Moderating Discussion

Meetings can often get bogged down in side trips, digressions, and distractions. Meeting leaders have to be willing to take charge by saying things like:

◆ "That's an interesting point, but let's table it for now."

◆ "How does that relate to our project?"

◆ "Excuse me, Fred, but let's give someone else a chance to speak."

◆ "We need to wrap up the discussion on this so we can move on to the next topic."

Effective team leaders get to know team members and their personalities. This knowledge enables them to better understand why team members do what they do. An important part of moderating discussion is to be aware of the negative team-member roles covered in Chapter 2 and how to deal with them. Preparing an agenda ahead of time and managing time are two other ways to effectively moderate discussion.

Managing Meeting Time

Meetings can be one of the biggest time robbers in any organization. Here are a few hints for managing meeting time:

◆ Always have specific starting and stopping times. Communicate those times to participants before the meeting.

◆ Stick to stated times. Start on time even if everyone isn't there. Don't be afraid to quit on time even if you are only halfway through the agenda. Doing so will communicate that you are serious about managing time.

◆ Divide the agenda into specific time blocks so members know how much time you have allotted for each item.

◆ Remind people of the time during the meeting. Comments such as "We only have 30 minutes left, so we need to pick up the pace" help keep people on track.

◆ If you take breaks, use unusual numbers, such as a 7- or 13-minute break. If you use the normal times, such as 10 or 15

3

Divide the agenda into specific time blocks so members know how much time you have allotted for each item.

minutes, people will tend to stretch them even longer. Always start again as soon as the designated break time is over.

- ◆ Limit distractions. Don't allow pagers or cellular phones in your meetings. Don't allow someone to interrupt with a message unless it is a real emergency.

- ◆ Don't hold meetings the first thing on Mondays or the last thing on Fridays.

- ◆ Don't hold meetings right after lunch. People may be late getting back or feel drowsy after they have eaten.

- ◆ Hold meetings that will end at the designated lunch time or the end of the workday. This will be an incentive to keep things moving.

- ◆ Don't be afraid to take charge. If it's your meeting, you have the most control over how time is managed.

Recording Minutes

Many teams have a designated secretary who is responsible for taking the minutes of team meetings and distributing them in a timely manner. A designated recording secretary allows participants to focus on what's happening during the meeting without having to take copious notes themselves.

Good meeting minutes can serve as a useful reference if questions arise about something the team did in the past.

Good meeting minutes can serve as a useful reference if questions arise about something the team did in the past. Minutes can also be used during a meeting if there is a question about something that was said or a decision that was made earlier in the meeting. A permanent set of minutes can also help a new member get up to speed on what the team has being doing. Likewise, the minutes can fill in missing gaps for team members who are absent from meetings.

If you have responsibility for team-meeting minutes, keep these points in mind:

- ◆ Include date, time, location, and names of attendees.

- ◆ Follow the flow of the meeting in chronological order.

◆ Use names of people who make pertinent comments. If the team operates using parliamentary procedure, be sure to include the names of those making and seconding motions.

◆ Document key decisions and who has responsibility for carrying out the decisions.

◆ Include a To-Do list generated during the meeting.

◆ Include the date, time, and location of the next meeting.

◆ Distribute the minutes as soon as possible, but not later than one week after the meeting.

Good meeting minutes serve as a history and can come in handy when preparing the team's final report.

Follow Up

Team leaders assume responsibility for following up with other team members between meetings. The amount and frequency will depend on their own experience as well as their knowledge of other team members. In the early stages, a team leader will follow up more frequently because he or she will likely be unfamiliar with how well other team members will meet their commitments and deadlines. After the team has been in place for a period of time, the leader will be able to back off more and give people more breathing space.

If you are a team member, you can help the process by taking the initiative to keep the team leader informed about your progress before he or she follows up with you. Taking the initiative is also a good way to show your support for the team. If you want to assume more of a leadership role in the future, taking the initiative when you are a team member is a good way to make a favorable impression.

Team leaders assume responsibility for following up with other team members between meetings.

3

Take a Moment

Rate your team meetings based on the following scale:

5 = Always
4 = Frequently
3 = About half the time
2 = Rarely
1 = Almost never

_____ We have a written agenda.
_____ We follow the agenda during the meeting.
_____ Progress reports are used to keep everyone informed.
_____ Discussion is controlled and focused.
_____ Meetings start and end on time.
_____ People arrive on time.
_____ Meeting minutes are useful.
_____ Minutes are received within a week after the meeting.
_____ The team leader follows up on commitments.
_____ Overall, I would say we have effective meetings.

What specifically can you do to help improve team meetings?

_____

_____

Team Ground Rules

"Bill, if you don't get that problem with the systems people resolved, you'll kill our chances for success."

"You're probably right, Pat. So what do you think I should do?"

"I don't know. That's your problem—not mine."

"It's also a team problem, Pat, and I need everyone's help in figuring out how to solve it."

"I don't know about everyone else, but I have enough problems of my own. If you can't handle it, Bill, maybe you shouldn't be on the team."

Bill and Pat have an obvious disagreement about who is responsible for solving problems—individual team members or the team as a whole. This disagreement could have been avoided if the team had established some ground rules in the beginning. Team ground rules are important because they:

◆ Create common expectations.

◆ Encourage desired behavior.

◆ Help a team self-manage itself.

It's best if the ground rules are developed by the team members themselves at the outset. The ground rules should also be in written form and a copy distributed to each team member. Here are nine ground rules for effective team management.

3

1. **Team problems are everyone's responsibility.**
   When the team wins, everyone wins. When the team loses, everyone loses. And when there are problems, everyone has to work together to solve those problems. Without this basic premise, the team really isn't functioning as a team. Instead, it becomes a group of people who are trying to solve their own problems and not taking advantage of the team synergy.

Team problems are everyone's responsibility.

2. **Every member participates.**
   Team members can't just be interested observers. Being on a team brings with it the responsibility to participate. Sometimes this may mean a member has to do a task he or she would rather not do. It may mean taking on new responsibilities and learning new things. Active team participation also requires being prepared for team meetings, team discussions, and team problem solving.

3. **All ideas deserve discussion.**
   Sometimes team members may come up with what appear at first glance to be wild ideas. That can be good, because it shows that people are willing to think outside the box. As long as the team member's idea is being put forth in a sincere, rather than frivolous, manner, it should be discussed. Many people scoffed at Bill Gates in the 1980s when he said that he envisioned companies where all employees had a computer on their desks. Fortunately, however, it was an idea that received further discussion.

4. **Team time belongs to the team.**
   Team meetings are not the time to catch up on reading memos, responding to e-mail, planning the next day, or returning phone calls. Like checking guns in the Old West, it's best to check cellular phones and pagers at the door—or at least to turn them off. Team members who give their attention to these distractions are delivering a not-so-subtle message that they have more important things to do.

5. **Derogatory comments or put-downs are not allowed.**
   Team members must treat each other with respect. Even comments that are meant in a friendly and playful manner can be taken the wrong way or misunderstood. Team members must show respect for each other and avoid doing or saying anything that minimizes the contributions of others. In a team setting, the Golden Rule of "treat others the way you want to be treated" is appropriate.

> **Team members must treat each other with respect.**

6. **Focus on one problem at a time.**
   Without focus, the team can lose its way and never solve a problem. A lack of focus can also lead to feelings of being overwhelmed by the sheer number of problems to be addressed. Focusing on one problem at a time can be difficult, because problems are often interrelated. The good news is that the solution to one problem opens up ideas that lead to the solution of other problems. The best approach is to focus on one problem at a time so team members' full energies and abilities are devoted to solving the problem at hand. Then the team can move on to the next issue.

7. **Meet team deadlines and commitments.**
   A car doesn't run smoothly if the spark plugs don't fire at the right times. Likewise, a team won't run smoothly if deadlines and commitments are missed. When one member fails to complete a task by a certain date, it can lead to problems for other team members. For example, if a team member doesn't complete a report on one part of a project, it can keep the team from making the necessary decisions so it can move forward. Likewise, team members who don't show up for meetings or who are constantly late can affect the productivity and morale of the rest of the team.

8. **Listen and ask questions.**
Team members aren't expected to know everything they need to know about a project in the beginning. Once they join the team, however, members must take active steps to learn about areas with which they are unfamiliar. One of the best ways to learn is to listen and ask questions during team meetings. Outside team meetings, members may need to get together one-on-one to find out more about what each one does. Team members who take time to listen and ask questions are likely to be better informed and contribute more to the team.

9. **Everyone supports team decisions.**
In an ideal world, there would be consensus on every decision made or action taken. Even on the most successful teams, however, there will likely be disagreement on the best way to do things. Team members often have to agree to disagree but still be willing to support each other in public. This means that when a decision, is made by the team, all members will support the decision, even if they don't necessarily agree with it. At the same time, those with reservations about a particular decision aren't expected to remain silent. When asked, they may express their concerns. In the end, however, they make sure that everyone understands that despite their reservations, they still support the team's decision.

3

Team members often have to agree to disagree but still be willing to support each other in public.

Take a Moment
Do You Play by the Ground Rules?
Read each of the following statements and circle the response that most accurately reflects what you do.

1. I am willing to help other team members solve problems.
   Yes   Sometimes   No

2. I actively participate in team discussions.
   Yes   Sometimes   No

3. I am willing to listen to other ideas, even when they seem far-fetched.
   Yes   Sometimes   No

Continued on next page

Take a Moment *(continued)*

4. I avoid doing nonteam work during team meetings.
   Yes   Sometimes   No

5. I avoid derogatory comments and put-downs of other team members, both in public and in private.
   Yes   Sometimes   No

6. I can focus on one problem at a time.
   Yes   Sometimes   No

7. I always meet my deadlines and commitments to the team.
   Yes   Sometimes   No

8. I listen and ask questions to increase my knowledge.
   Yes   Sometimes   No

9. I support team decisions in public, even when I disagree.
   Yes   Sometimes   No

Total: Yes _____   Sometimes _____   No _____

What specific things can you do to move your Sometimes and No responses to the Yes column?

_____

_____

_____

Chapter Summary

A team's charter establishes its purpose and goals, identifies any constraints or parameters, and explains how the team will function. Team meetings provide an opportunity for members to connect with each other to keep informed on the status of various assignments. A set of ground rules helps create common expectations, encourages desired behavior, and helps a team self-manage itself.

Self-Check: Chapter 3 Review

Complete each of the following statements. Suggested answers are on page 115.

1. A team charter is a _____ document that seeks to lay the groundwork for dealing with issues and situations that may arise in the future.

2. Teams need to have a sense of purpose that is reflected in their _____ or _____.

3. All teams need a _____ to provide a sense of identity.

4. What five items are recommended by the author to be included in a team-meeting agenda?

    a. _____

    b. _____

    c. _____

    d. _____

    e. _____

5. All meetings should have a specific _____ and _____ time.

6. At the latest, meeting minutes should be distributed within _____ _____ after the meeting.

7. List three reasons why team ground rules are important.

    a. _____

    b. _____

    c. _____

Chapter *Four*

Becoming a Team Leader

Chapter Objectives

▶ Describe what an effective team facilitator/leader does.

▶ Identify facilitator/leader responsibilities.

"**D**id you hear who our team leader is going to be?"

"No. Who's it gonna be?"

"You and me."

"Both of us? I'm confused."

"Don't be. It's been decided that all members of the team are going to share the responsibility for being team leader."

Team leadership roles are not restricted to a select few. In teams that are formed for extended periods of time, the leadership role often rotates from one person to the next. Even in teams with a shorter life span, there may be times when the team leader will be absent, and someone else has to take charge. One of the real benefits of being on a team is learning about and being given the opportunity to assume a leadership position. This chapter will help you prepare for assuming leadership roles and responsibilities on your team.

An effective team facilitator makes it easy (or at least possible) for the team to function well.

The word *facilitator* has also been used to describe team leadership. The term is drawn from Latin roots and means *one who makes things easy.* An effective team facilitator makes it easy (or at least possible) for the team to function well. The terms *facilitator* and *leader* are used interchangeably in this chapter because they both describe the expectations members have of those in charge—to smooth the way for team members and to provide leadership.

What Team Leaders Do

Individuals who serve as team leaders need to provide an on-going sense of direction and purpose to team members. There are four techniques that can help you do this more effectively:

◆ Focusing on team mission and performance goals

◆ Developing mutual accountability

◆ Demonstrating a willingness to work alongside other team members

◆ Reflecting a team-oriented attitude

Focusing on Team Mission and Performance Goals

Effective leaders regularly remind team members of their common purpose. By focusing on their team's purpose, team leaders keep their teams moving forward toward their goals. They also know that team performance is more important than individual achievement. They use the "we" approach when talking about the team. When credit is given, it is given to the team and its members, not to the leader.

Most of us expect a person who is called the leader to take charge. The best team leaders, however, are careful not to push their ideas on the team, especially in the early stages of development. They are aware that other members may interpret the things they say or do as leaders as carrying more weight, so they constantly reassure members: "It's not what I think, but what the team thinks that's important."

Effective facilitators/leaders work to minimize their influence on specifics but maximize their influence on keeping the team focused on its common purpose. They know that in the final analysis, it is the accomplishment of mission and goals that matters most.

> **Individuals who serve as team leaders need to provide an ongoing sense of direction and purpose to team members.**

4

Developing Mutual Accountability

Leaders and members have to hold each other accountable for their actions. This is a critical and difficult challenge for most teams. Team accountability requires living up to the promises (spoken and unspoken) that members make to each other—that by agreeing to be a part of the team, each person will do his or her share.

Developing mutual accountability often comes back to the leader's ability to keep the team focused on its common purpose. If the team is truly focused on its mission and performance goals, members will hold each other accountable because they want the team to succeed. By contrast, a half-hearted commitment to the team's purpose can lead to a "who cares?" attitude about missed deadlines and assignments. Mutual accountability depends on how well the leader is able to communicate and convince team members of the worthiness of its common purpose.

> **Everyone on the team has to be willing to work— including the leader.**

Demonstrating a Willingness to Work Alongside Other Team Members

Everyone on the team has to be willing to work—including the leader. Effective leaders are active participants in the work of the team. They don't just sit back and let others do the work. They take on their share of assignments roughly equal to that of other team members. Their motto is "No job is too big or too small."

Effective leaders also use team meetings as an opportunity to demonstrate the importance of getting work done in a timely manner. Their reports are always on time, crisp, clear, and to the point. Team facilitators demonstrate what they expect from all team members. This approach pays benefits in more team cohesiveness and commitment to the team's mission and performance goals.

Reflecting a Team-Oriented Attitude

When we say someone has a "good attitude" or a "bad attitude," what are we really describing? An *attitude* is an internal state similar to an emotion—the only way we could ever really know another person's attitude is if we could read his or her mind. When we describe someone's attitude, what we are really describing is that person's *behavior.* If someone smiles, we think she has a good attitude. If someone frowns, we look on him as having a bad attitude—but he might just have a toothache.

Certain behaviors can reflect a team-oriented attitude. Here are a few techniques that team leaders should try:

◆ Smile when people make positive contributions. A smile is an outward sign that things are going well and one that effective team leaders use often.

◆ Take unbiased action. Set aside any biases you have and look only at the contributions of team members—not their ethnicity, social standing, department, or level in the organization.

◆ Use a "we" approach. Emphasize the word *we* instead of *I* and *you.* Problems and issues are ours, not yours—they belong to the entire team.

◆ Treat members with respect. Give team members who want to make suggestions and comments ample opportunity to do so. Value all team-member views as contributions to the work of the team.

◆ Do not blame individuals. When something goes wrong, don't single out individuals for blame or punishment. Effective team leaders honestly believe that any failure is due to what the team did—not the result of one person's actions.

4

Take a Moment

List specific steps you can take when you assume the role of team leader to develop the following techniques.

1. Keep the focus on team mission and performance goals.

_____

_____

Continued on next page

Take a Moment *(continued)*

2. Develop mutual accountability.

_____

_____

3. Demonstrate a willingness to work alongside other team members.

_____

_____

4. Reflect a team-oriented attitude.

_____

_____

Assuming Leadership Responsibilities

Mastering the techniques just described will help you assume the responsibilities of team leadership. Some of these responsibilities include:

◆ Focusing on results

◆ Building commitment and confidence

◆ Creating opportunities for others

◆ Providing structure

◆ Encouraging participation

◆ Avoiding the manipulation of others

◆ Managing external relationships

◆ Keeping management informed

◆ Bringing new members into the team

By taking on these responsibilities, team leaders provide additional support for team members and direction for their work.

Focusing on Results

Team leaders ask questions like:

◆ "What are we accomplishing?"

◆ "Are we moving closer to our goal?"

◆ "How will that help us succeed?"

◆ "What do we need to do next?"

All these questions are designed to keep the team focused on results so it achieves its common purpose.

Effective team facilitators know that the team will only be seen as successful when results are achieved. It doesn't matter what they do along the way if they don't achieve specific results. The leaders who succeed are those who believe in their people and their ability to get results. They communicate their beliefs as often as possible so that the team remains focused and on the right track.

Building Commitment and Confidence

Each member determines his or her own level of commitment to the team's purpose. The leader's role is to create an environment that supports that commitment. A positive environment exists when people believe that their ideas are respected, receive recognition for their contributions, and feel good about what they are doing. Commitment is also generated when team members buy in to the team's mission and performance goals. People are also more likely to be committed when leaders provide the support and resources needed to get the job done.

Leaders build confidence in team members who may be lacking it. Many of the same behaviors that build commitment also build confidence. One of the most powerful confidence builders is positive feedback that lets team members know they are succeeding. Effective team leaders go out of their way to take a personal interest in the people on the team, putting the needs of team members above their own.

4

Effective team facilitators know that the team will only be seen as successful when results are achieved.

Creating Opportunities for Others

Effective team
leaders give
members
assignments
that will
challenge and
stretch them to
do something
new.

Team performance is not possible if the team facilitator takes all the plum assignments. An important facilitator responsibility is to give other team members an opportunity to develop their skills. One way to do this is to give members assignments that will challenge and stretch them to do something new. If a task is assigned to someone who already knows how to do that task, that person won't learn anything new. If the team is under a short deadline, giving people assignments they can easily do may be the most practical approach. However, the team and the team members will be better served if, at least once in a while, members are given a challenging assignment.

Another approach is to develop smaller teams within the team. For example, a person who has experience in a particular area can be teamed with someone inexperienced who would benefit from learning about that area. The less-experienced person takes the lead on the project, while the experienced person serves as a mentor, providing general guidance and answering questions. During the assignment, the mentor is always available to provide guidance—but not to take over the assignment.

Providing Structure

A well-organized team is able to focus on results and purpose because it doesn't have to waste valuable time figuring things out as it goes along. Effective team leaders provide the structure for success in a variety of ways, some of which have been previously discussed:

◆ Working with the team to develop a team charter

◆ Holding team meetings that follow an agenda

◆ Using a standardized format for reports

◆ Establishing a set of team ground rules that everyone is expected to follow

◆ Having a consistent method of dealing with conflicts and issues

Encouraging Participation

When all team members participate, they share a sense of ownership in what the team is doing and trying to achieve. It is the team leader's responsibility to ensure that all team members participate and contribute.

The starting point for encouraging participation is to clearly communicate expectations to team members as soon as the team is formed. One way to encourage participation during team meetings is to ask questions of team members who may seem reluctant to get involved. Another approach is to give team members specific assignments that require them to be actively involved in the work of the team. The team leader's own example of full participation will signal to other members the importance of getting involved.

> When all team members participate, they share a sense of ownership in what the team is doing and trying to achieve.

4

Avoiding the Manipulation of Others

Effective team facilitators avoid hidden agendas. If team members suspect the leader is trying to lead them to a predetermined solution, they will not be open in sharing their ideas.

Effective team facilitators always keep in mind that their objective is to help the team achieve its mission—not to push their own agendas. Comments such as, "If that's what you wanted, why didn't you just say so and save us all a lot of time?" indicate a team facilitator who is perceived as a manipulator. Team members also need to be able to trust the team facilitator to maintain confidentiality when requested to do so.

Managing External Relationships

Team leaders are usually expected to manage the team's contacts with others in the organization. Team members must know they can depend on the leader to promote the team and its importance. For example, if a department head goes to a team leader to complain about how much time an employee is spending on the team's work, the team leader can't cave in. Instead, the team leader has to be able to clearly communicate to the department head the team's mission and goals and why they are important.

Managing external relationships also requires having a knowledge of who to go to for support and resources. Effective team leaders know which direction to point team members so they have the support and resources necessary to accomplish their assigned tasks. The leader may also be able to pave the way for the team member. For example, the team leader may contact a department head and tell her that a team member will be contacting her for specific information.

Keeping Management Informed

Since many teams are formed at the request of management, the team facilitator is responsible for keeping management informed. This may mean attending meetings and providing updates on the team's progress. It may require submitting written reports on a regular basis. Effective team facilitators don't sugarcoat bad news or make good news sound too good to be true. They are always open and honest in their evaluation of the team's performance and how it is portrayed to management.

The best team facilitators make sure management is kept informed— even if they don't ask for it.

The best team facilitators make sure management is kept informed—even if they don't ask for it. They operate on the assumption that "the best surprise is no surprise." They take a proactive approach and allow management the opportunity to bring up any issues or concerns early in the team process.

Bringing New Members into the Team

Very few teams end their assignments with the same members as when they started. People get promoted, leave organizations, transfer to other departments, or just plain quit. When this happens, a new member must join the team to pick up the slack. It becomes the team leader's responsibility to ensure that new members are oriented to the team.

The goal of the orientation is to bring the new person up to speed as quickly as possible so that the team's work can go on with minimal interruption. Here are some things that can be helpful when orienting a new team member:

◆ Introduce the member to the rest of the team and have team members introduce themselves.

- Give the new member a chance to tell the team about himself or herself.

- Provide copies of the minutes of all previous meetings.

- Assign the new person to a "buddy" who can answer questions and fill in the details.

- Give the new member an immediate assignment so he or she can make a contribution to the team.

- Send out a written communication to those who need to know that you have a new member on the team and what his or her responsibilities will be.

- Make yourself available to answer questions.

Taking a little bit of time up front can ease the new person onto the team and help him or her quickly become productive.

4

Take a Moment
Can You Be an Effective Team Leader?
Do you have what it takes to lead a team? Use the following scale to rate your current level of knowledge and skills.
4 = Definitely can do it
3 = Probably can do it
2 = Not sure
1 = Can't do it at this time; needs work

_____	Focus on results
_____	Build commitment and confidence
_____	Create opportunities for others
_____	Provide structure
_____	Encourage participation
_____	Avoid manipulating others
_____	Manage external relationships
_____	Keep management informed
_____	Orient new members to the team

For any items you rated as a 1 or 2, write a personal action plan to increase your knowledge and ability.

_____

_____

Chapter Summary

Team leadership roles often rotate among team members who have the ability to:

◆ Keep the team focused on its mission and performance goals.

◆ Develop mutual accountability.

◆ Demonstrate a willingness to work alongside other team members.

◆ Reflect a team-oriented attitude.

These techniques serve as the foundation for carrying out the specific leadership responsibilities outlined in this chapter, which provide additional support to the team and its members.

Self-Check: Chapter 4 Review

Complete each of the following statements. Check your answers on page 115.

1. The word *facilitator* means one who makes _____ _____.

2. Individuals who assume a leadership role have to be able to see the _____ _____ of the team's purpose.

3. Match the following Techniques and Strategies of team leaders.

Techniques

_____   Focus on team's mission
_____   Develop mutual accountability
_____   Work alongside team members
_____   Team-oriented attitude

Strategies

  a. Keep promises and commitments
  b. Do not blame individuals
  c. Avoid pushing own ideas
  d. Believe "No job is too small"

4. The team leader's role is to create an _____ that supports team members' commitment.

5. One of the ways a team leader can encourage participation is to clearly communicate _____ in the beginning.

6. The best team leaders take a _____ approach to keeping management informed of the team's progress.

Chapter *Five*

Working Together

Chapter Objectives

▶ Describe methods for getting team members involved.

▶ Manage and resolve conflict.

▶ Build trust among team members.

▶ List ways to get the team unstuck when things bog down.

Cathy and Steve were on the way to the conference room for a team meeting. Their team had been working together for about a year, and the group was close to achieving its goals.

"This has been one of the best teams I've ever been on," Cathy said as they turned down the hall.

"Yeah, it has been pretty good, hasn't it?" Steve agreed.

"I can think of several reasons why," Cathy observed. "First, we shared the role of leadership, so we've all had a chance to be involved in guiding the team."

Steve nodded. "I like the way everyone's been willing to get involved, whether they're acting as team leader or team member," he said.

When a team is first formed, the members generally have high expectations.

"There haven't been any major conflicts either," said Cathy. "Those that have come up have been resolved pretty well."

"That's because we trust each other," Steve said.

Are Cathy and Steve living in a dream world? Could a team really function that well? Why not? When a team is first formed, the members generally have high expectations. They want the team to succeed, and they want to have an enjoyable experience. While it may not be smooth sailing all the time, a team should be able to function in a positive manner most of the time. The key is learning to work together.

In this chapter, you'll learn some of the methods used by successful teams. Remember, whether it's your turn to be the designated team leader, or you are in your role as a contributing team member, your knowledge and understanding of these methods will help you and your team succeed.

Getting Team Members Involved

Successful team facilitators understand that their success is often in inverse proportion to the amount of time they spend talking. As we learned in the last chapter, they don't push their ideas on the team; instead, they involve team members and get input from them. Let's look at four things that can get team members involved:

♦ Asking questions

♦ Brainstorming

♦ Guiding discussions

♦ Avoiding and overcoming *groupthink*

Asking Questions

The easiest way to get team members involved is to ask appropriate questions, then listen to what they have to say. There are four types of questions that can be used to keep the discussion flowing. These questions work whether you are facilitating the discussion or being an active team member.

♦ **Open questions**—The best way to encourage involvement is to ask questions that cannot be answered with a yes, a no, or a brief factual response. Open questions typically begin with words like *what, why, how, what if,* or *tell me about.* The objective is to get members to open up and contribute to the discussion. An open question is often the best place to begin a discussion. Some open questions you might use are:

■ "What do you think about the team's mission?"

■ "Why do you think we should adopt that strategy?"

> **Successful team facilitators understand that their success is often in inverse proportion to the amount of time they spend talking.**

5

67

- "How could we accomplish that in the time we have available?"

- "That's sounds interesting. Tell me more about it."

Open questions usually are not directed to a specific person. They are posed to the whole team, and anyone can respond.

◆ **Direct Questions**—Direct questions are directed to a specific team member. Generally, a direct question is an open question with a person's name attached at the end: "What do you think about the team's mission, Jim?" The name is put at the end on purpose. If the person's name comes first, the other participants may stop listening since they know the question isn't coming their way. Also, if you ask an open question and no one responds, you can turn it into a direct question by simply adding a name.

Use direct questions only when you know the person you are calling on has something to contribute. Don't use direct questions to embarrass or put someone on the spot. Doing so only discourages participation—not only does the person you put on the spot feel uncomfortable, but so do the other team members.

> **Use direct questions only when you know the person you are calling on has something to contribute.**

◆ **Reverse Questions**—Reverse questions are just what the name implies—they are questions that are reversed back to the person who asked them. Remember, when you are facilitating the team, you want the team members to do most of the talking. You may be flattered when you are asked a question and be tempted to give your answer. However, giving an answer can stifle the discussion if others think that what you (as team facilitator) say carries more weight than it actually does. When reversing a question, it's a good idea to say something so it does not appear that you are unwilling to answer questions. Here are some lead-ins that you might use when reversing a question:

- "I'm not sure what I think about that. What do you think?"

- "That's an interesting question. What would you do?"

- "I have an idea, but I'd like to hear yours first. What do you think we should do?"

The purpose of reverse questions is to keep the focus on team members so they feel more a part of the team.

◆ **Referral Questions**—Referral questions are similar to reverse questions. The difference is that instead of reversing the question back to the person who asked it, you refer it to the team as a whole or to another team member. Sometimes you will get a question that you know someone else on the team can answer. Or you may want to involve a person who has been quiet (don't refer the questions if it will put the person on the spot). Like reverse questions, team leaders use referrals to keep the spotlight on the team and off of themselves. Here's how a referral might be used in a team meeting:

Larry (to the team leader):
I think we can have the new system up and running within 30 days, don't you?

Team leader:
How does 30 days sound to the rest of you?

Bill:
I think it's possible—if we get a few breaks.

Team leader:
How about you, Carol?

The team leader first referred the question to the whole team and then to a specific person. Notice that the second referral question is like the direct question in that the person's name is added at the end.

Being able to ask effective questions is one of the methods you can use, even when you aren't in the team facilitator role, to keep discussion moving and to involve other team members. Asking questions is only part of the task.

On the flip side is the ability to listen. Unless you listen to what people say, you won't be able to ask good follow-up questions. It's impossible to reverse or refer a question if you didn't hear the original question yourself. It is also difficult to keep a discussion moving if you don't give your full attention to what is being said.

5

Successful team members have mastered the art of *active listening.* Active listening lets others know that you are really hearing what they are saying. One of the best ways to convey that you are listening is to restate what the other person said—either in their own words or by paraphrasing. Other things you can do to indicate that you are actively listening are:

> Active listening lets others know that you are really hearing what they are saying.

- ◆ **Use positive body language**—make eye contact with the person speaking and lean forward. Don't cross your arms or frown, as it may appear you are not receptive to what is being said.

- ◆ **Eliminate distractions**—focus your full attention on the person speaking. Don't look at your watch, shuffle papers, or look at someone else.

- ◆ **Avoid making judgments**—try to remain neutral. Don't indicate whether you agree or disagree with the person speaking. Let that person know that you will consider her or his point of view.

Take a Moment

Think about the next team discussion you are going to facilitate. Do a little preparation and consider some of the questions you might ask your team.

What are some open questions you might use to start the discussion?

_____

_____

If you don't get a response, to whom might you direct the questions?

_____

_____

Continued on next page

Take a Moment *(continued)*

What types of questions do you anticipate the group will ask you? To whom could you refer the question?

_____

_____

What do you need to do to improve your listening skills?

_____

_____

5

Brainstorming

Brainstorming is a technique that teams use often in the course of working together to accomplish their mission and performance goals. Brainstorming can be used at various stages in the problem-solving process or anytime there is a need to generate many ideas from the team. Some of the benefits of brainstorming are:

◆ It encourages involvement.

◆ It gets team energy flowing.

◆ It requires few props (flip chart and markers).

◆ It allows a lot to be accomplished in a short amount of time.

◆ It's generally fun.

The key to brainstorming is to maintain a nonjudgmental atmosphere so that all ideas are given value. The steps in the brainstorming process are:

1. Introduce the purpose and process.

2. Select a recorder to write ideas on the flip chart. This will allow you to focus your attention on directing the brainstorming session.

> **The key to brainstorming is to maintain a nonjudgmental atmosphere so that all ideas are given value.**

3. Set up a flip chart where it can be seen.

4. Clarify and define the issue or problem to be discussed.

5. Review the ground rules. This includes specifying any time constraints; cautioning members not to evaluate or make judgments of ideas; go for quantity, not quality; and encouraging freewheeling.

6. Ask people to start contributing ideas and suggestions. Have the recorder write the ideas on the flip chart. Keep going until the team runs out of ideas or time.

7. Review and combine ideas. Now is the time for discussion. Eliminate unrealistic or unusable ideas. Keep those that address the issue or problem.

8. Develop a plan. Now is the time to decide what to do with the results of the brainstorming. The team has invested time in the process, so make sure you use their ideas.

Take a Moment

What are some issues that your team needs to brainstorm? Write down as many as you can think of.

_____

_____

_____

Now go to another team member and see if he or she can add to your list. Write the additions below.

_____

_____

_____

Continued on next page

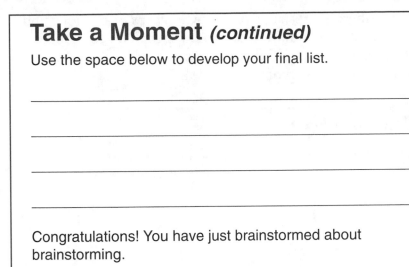

Take a Moment *(continued)*

Use the space below to develop your final list.

_____

_____

_____

_____

Congratulations! You have just brainstormed about brainstorming.

Guiding Discussions

Much of a team's time together will be spent in discussion. When several people are involved, a discussion can easily get off track. Whenever this happens, the team leader has to bring the group back into focus. Here are some techniques for guiding group discussions:

◆ Keep the topic in front of everyone. Write it on a flip chart page or chalk board if either is available. If you know the topic before the team meets, put it on the written agenda.

◆ State the topic and ask each person to think individually about a response.

◆ Use a round-robin method to get responses from team members. Each person contributes one idea, then the next person has a turn. Continue in this fashion until all the ideas have been given.

◆ Ask another team member to help you monitor the discussion. This second person can give you a signal or say something that indicates the discussion needs to get back on track.

◆ Set time limits for the discussion—and stick to them. When time is up, conclude the discussion. After you do this a couple of times, team members will know you are serious.

5

Team members appreciate a person who keeps discussions under control and does not allow one or a few people to monopolize the time. A well-managed discussion can help keep teams working together to accomplish their mission.

Take a Moment

How are you at handling discussions? List below any techniques mentioned in this chapter that you want to try.

_____

_____

_____

_____

_____

_____

Avoiding and Overcoming "Groupthink"

Groupthink sets in when team members put the views of the team above their individual ideas.

Although teams need to work together, cooperation can get carried too far. *Groupthink* sets in when team members put the views of the team above their individual ideas. Groupthink is normally not a deliberate action. Members simply rationalize any concerns they have as being misguided or irrelevant. As a result, they remain silent and the group (team) continues to think all is well. You have probably experienced this phenomenon at some time or another.

■ **Example:** At a team meeting, everyone seemingly agrees with a team decision. Then the decision is carried out, and it doesn't work. Later, some team members say they had reservations all along, but they didn't want to rock the boat.

Here are some techniques that can be used to overcome groupthink:

◆ Demonstrate and encourage critical thinking. Let everyone know that critical analysis is valued.

◆ Appoint a devil's advocate. This person takes on the role of challenging the team whenever it seems they are too quick to agree.

◆ Encourage everyone to participate. Don't let team members withdraw from a discussion. They may have a contrary view that needs to be heard.

◆ Have a second-look meeting. Don't rush to implement an idea. Let team members mull it over for a while and then discuss it again in the future. Perhaps they will think of other ideas in the meantime.

Overcoming groupthink is not easy—especially since one of the basic ideas of being part of a team is to work together. Make sure your team practices the techniques listed above so that real agreement (not groupthink) is the end result of team discussions.

5

Take a Moment

Have you seen any signs of groupthink on your team? If so, what can you do to reduce the chance of it happening again?

_____

_____

_____

_____

Managing and Resolving Conflict

Conflict—the mere mention of the word can make some people feel uneasy. A team without some conflict, however, probably isn't accomplishing very much. If there are never any differences of opinion, it may be that the team has settled into groupthink. When a team discusses a specific problem, conflicts might occur regarding the source of the problem, the best solutions to the problem, or who will be responsible for taking action.

> **Handled properly, conflict can actually help a team make better, more informed decisions.**

No matter what you do, conflict is bound to occur in your team sooner or later. The key is use that conflict to your advantage. Conflict can be an opportunity to get ideas out in the open and ensure that the team looks at all sides of an issue. Handled properly, conflict can actually help a team make better, more informed decisions.

Conflict-Resolution Process

Here's a four-step process your team can use to resolve conflict:

1. Acknowledge the conflict.

2. Discuss the conflict.

3. Agree on a solution.

4. Monitor results.

Let's look at how to apply these steps to resolve a conflict among team members.

Acknowledge the Conflict

Before your team can resolve a conflict, it has to admit that there is a conflict, as in the following case study. Ted is the team leader.

Case Study

Ted:
We need to present our findings to management next Tuesday.

Paul:
I hope they like what we do this time better than the last presentation we did.

Joan:
It wasn't the presentation—it was the message they didn't like.

Cathy:
I don't think they liked either one very much.

John:
It was a technical nightmare! Everything that could go wrong did go wrong. We need to stick to paper reports and forget that computer stuff.

Joan:
You're just paranoid. The problem wasn't the computer—it was that we didn't have enough time to prepare.

Cathy:
Let's do whatever is easiest.

Paul:
Unfortunately, the easiest may not be the best.

John:
But the easiest might be good enough.

Joan:
I'm not so sure about that.

Ted:
It sounds like we have difference of opinion on what we should do.

All:
At least we can all agree on that.

Discuss the Conflict

Discussing the conflict can lead to even more conflict—unless you make an effort to keep everyone focused and maintain a civil atmosphere. Here are some strategies to follow when discussing the conflict:

◆ **Give everyone a chance to speak.** Conflicts may seem larger than they really are if a few members do all the talking. Make sure everyone is drawn into the discussion.

◆ **Focus on the conflict—not the person.** Don't let personal attacks overshadow honest disagreement. The goal is to resolve the conflict, not change the person.

◆ **Give equal time to all points of view.** Better decisions can be made if team members have a chance to hear all sides of an issue before they make up their minds.

◆ **Agree to disagree.** Most people can "live with" a decision and support it even if they don't agree with it 100 percent— as long as they have had a chance to air their concerns.

Let's see how this works in our case study:

Case Study

Ted:
Let's discuss the situation. We need to resolve it so we can get started preparing the presentation.

Joan:
I think we should use the computer graphics again. They add a lot to the presentation.

John:
But what if it doesn't work—like last time?

Cathy:
Let's prepare paper copies of the computer graphics that we can hand out.

Paul:
Now there's an idea. If the computer goes down, we'll still have the graphics available.

Ted:
What do you think, John? Would that make you feel more comfortable.

John:
I can live with it—as long as I don't have to run the computer.

Joan:
I'll be glad to take responsibility for the computer operation.

Ted:
Anyone object to that?

All:
No.

Ted:
What other concerns do you have?

Paul:
Well, since you asked, I also think we should have more than one person making the presentation.

Cathy:
You didn't like my presentation?

Paul:
You did fine last time. But I think having multiple presenters can make a more interesting presentation.

Ted:
What do you think about that, Joan?

At this point, Ted would continue to guide the discussion until the team had discussed all their concerns about the presentation. He would also try to reach agreement on what the team will do.

Agree on a Solution

The team leader should summarize the discussion whenever there appears to be agreement among team members. This ensures that everyone knows what the solution is and allows for any other discussion that may be needed, as we can see in our case study:

Ted:
So we have agreed to use the computer again and to provide paper copies to those who attend. Is everyone in agreement with that?

Joan:
Sounds good.

Cathy:
Let's try it.

Paul:
I'll go along with that.

Ted:
How about you, John?

Case Study

5

John:
I'm still not crazy about using the computer, but it sounds like we have a backup plan this time. I'm willing to try it.

Ted:
Then it's agreed. And we also agreed that each of us will make a part of the presentation.

Monitor Results

The last step in the process is to monitor what happens after the team puts in plan into action. Let's return for a final look at our case study:

Case Study

Ted:
How can we monitor our results?

John:
If it works, it works. If it doesn't, it doesn't. Seems pretty straight-forward to me.

Joan:
That's true. But we might want to discuss the presentation afterward.

Paul:
I think we should have a short debriefing session. We can discuss what went well. And if there are still problems to figure out, we can discuss how to fix them.

Cathy:
If we do it right after the presentation, while it's still fresh in our minds, we'll have a better discussion.

Ted:
The presentation is supposed to end at 4:30. Can everyone stay until 5:30 to debrief?

Conflict is natural and is not a sign that there is something wrong with your team.

Things may not always go as smoothly for your team as they did in the case study. However, using the four-step process can help resolve conflicts and keep your team moving forward. Remember, conflict is natural and is not a sign that there is something wrong with your team. The best teams use conflict to their advantage—rather than ignoring it and hoping it will go away. As shown in the case study, conflict can lead to different ways of doing things and get everyone to agree on taking a particular course of action.

Building Trust

When team members trust each other, they work together well and are able to work through conflict situations. Trust is critical, because the level of trust among members affects how ideas are generated, how decisions are made, and how conflicts are resolved. To manage conflict effectively, as well as do all the other things a team must do together, all members must act in a way that builds trust.

Trust Builders

Team members build trust by their behavior in team meetings and in other settings. Effective team members know there is no single thing you can do to build trust and they do their best to practice the six trust builders listed below.

◆ **Control your tongue.** Sarcasm at team meetings and criticism of other team members can lower your image in the eyes of other team members. Words are important. Even things you say in jest can be taken wrong or seriously by others. As they say, "Engage your brain first, then your mouth."

◆ **Be honest.** Level with team members. If you think an idea is bad, don't be afraid to say so. Likewise, if you think something is good, say so. Don't say something you really don't believe or stretch the truth. Always level with team members if you want to gain their respect and trust. And most importantly, don't say one thing in a team meeting and something else outside the meeting.

◆ **Keep your word.** Nothing builds trust like being dependable and reliable. People want to know that you will do what you say, when you say you will do it. Be the kind of person that others can count on, and you'll find yourself a trusted team member.

◆ **Act from facts.** Everyone has an opinion. Unfortunately, many of those opinions are based on erroneous information. If you are giving an opinion, say so. Problems are created when people state their opinions as if they were factual. Make it a point to base your comments and actions on the facts.

> Team members build trust by their behavior in team meetings and in other settings.

5

81

♦ **Practice the golden rule.** You can't go wrong if you treat others the way you want to be treated. People trust those who will not do something that they themselves would consider unacceptable. Ask yourself, "How would I like to be treated in this situation?" Your honest response can serve as your guide to the most appropriate action.

♦ **Support the team.** Be a cheerleader for your team. Talk up the team outside of meetings. Be complimentary about team members and the work of the team whenever you have the chance. Even if you don't agree with everything that the team decides in private, it's your responsibility to support the team in public.

Trust Survey

Do you think team members trust you? Use the survey below to determine if your team members view you as trustworthy. Give a copy of the survey to each person on your team. Have them fill in their responses and return their surveys to you. Tell them they don't have to put their names on the survey. Have your immediate supervisor (or team leader) complete the survey. Also, have any people who report to you fill out a survey as well.

The process of having others complete the survey is called 360-degree feedback because it allows you to get feedback from all those with whom you work. Be sure to complete the survey too, and then compare your perceptions of your trust-building skills with the perceptions of the other people who fill out the survey.

Trust Survey

_____   _____
            Person being rated   Date

Relationship to person being rated:
Team Member _____   Team Leader _____   Direct Report _____

Directions: Place a check mark in the column that best describes the normal behavior of the person being rated.

	Always	Sometimes	Never
Controls tongue	___	___	___
Is honest with others	___	___	___
Keeps his or her word	___	___	___
Acts from facts, rather than opinions	___	___	___
Practices the golden rule	___	___	___
Supports the team in public	___	___	___

Comments:

_____

_____

_____

5

Take a Moment

After you have completed your survey and compared your own perceptions with those who completed surveys, use the space below to write a personal action plan. List any actions you need to take to improve your trustworthiness.

_____

_____

_____

_____

Getting the Team Unstuck

When a team is functioning well, it seems like nothing can slow it down. Most teams, however, will occasionally reach a point at which they get stuck—they run into a major obstacle, get distracted by something, or just can't seem to get focused. The result can be frustration and a lack of progress. In the worst-case scenario, when a team is unable to get back on track, the best solution may be to dissolve the team. Before making that decision, here are some approaches to consider to get a team unstuck.

Revisit the Basics

The starting point is to revisit the basics: the team mission and performance goals, the team charter, team-member selections, team-member roles and responsibilities, and ground rules. In short, the team may need to rethink why it was formed and the approaches it has been taking.

Sometimes a team may work for several months on its assignment and then decide that perhaps it hadn't accurately described its mission. Or after a few meetings, the team may decide that it doesn't have the right members or needs some additional expertise to accomplish its mission. The team that is stuck may need to stop working on its assignment and take time to have a special team meeting to reexamine its basic assumptions. Once any needed changes are made, the team can resume its work with a new focus and commitment.

Go for Small Wins

Nothing helps a team more than winning. When times get tough, even the smallest win can seem significant. For example, the act of going back and rethinking the team mission and performance goals (revisiting the basics) can be viewed as a win if everyone gets refocused. A change in the performance goal, such as reaching the objective in nine months rather than six months, can take the pressure off and be viewed as a win by the team.

Another approach is to reassign team members to a specific problem until it is solved. For example, one person has a specific assignment and the team can't move ahead until his assignment is completed. Instead of waiting, several team members help the other team member until the assignment is completed.

Try New Approaches

Sometimes teams get in a rut because they do the same thing over and over. For example, every time an issue comes up, no matter how big or small, the team automatically starts brainstorming. Or the same members get the same type of assignments every time. Phil always gets the human resources issues, and Mary always gets the accounting issues. Perhaps a switch of responsibilities can bring fresh thinking to an issue and get the team unstuck.

> A switch of responsibilities can bring fresh thinking to an issue and get the team unstuck.

Bring in Outsiders

Sometimes it may help to bring in outsiders who can give the team a different perspective. Some teams have found that bringing in an outside facilitator to work with the team can help get it moving again. The key is for the facilitator to help the team get its attention focused on its mission and performance goals.

Other teams have found that providing some specialized training to team members can be helpful. For example, a half-day session on problem-solving techniques might help a team that is having difficulty with that part of its task. In order for the training to be successful, it must provide the team with real tools that it can put into practice immediately. Simply talking in theoretical terms and models won't help get a team unstuck—it may, in fact, get them stuck deeper.

Change Team Members or Leaders

Many teams avoid getting stuck by making frequent changes in team members or leaders. New members can bring a new perspective and new ideas to the table. Removing members who are not contributing can also be necessary at times. Changes in membership can also result in some loss of productivity, but in the end, this concession may be worth it to get the team moving again.

Throughout this book, the premise has been that anyone can function in the role of team leader. Rotating the leadership role among team members is one way to keep a fresh perspective and keep from getting stuck. A new leader may not get the team unstuck, however, if the new leader simply does what the previous leader did. New leaders have to introduce new ways of doing things. A team that changes leaders but stays stuck is no better off than it was before.

5

Take a Moment

Consider the following scenarios. Based on the options just discussed and your own experience, what action would you recommend?

■ Your team worked hard to establish a set of six-month objectives. After three months, it's obvious they won't be met, and team members are becoming frustrated.

_____

_____

■ Your team keeps coming up with the same solutions to the same problems and keeps getting the same results. Nothing seems to be working.

_____

_____

■ Your team has been working on specific performance goals ever since it was formed. Now it appears that the goals will be achieved, but in the end it will make little difference.

_____

_____

Chapter Summary

Effective team leaders recognize the importance of getting all team members involved in the team's activities and decisions. They also recognize that conflict does occur, but that it can be used in a constructive manner. One way to reduce conflict is to have an atmosphere where members' behavior leads them to trust each other. This feeling of trust is helpful if a team gets bogged down, because members can work together to take specific actions to get the team unstuck.

Self-Check: Chapter 5 Review

Complete each of the following statements. Check your answers on page 116.

1. List and describe the four types of questions that can be used to keep a discussion moving.

   a. _____

   b. _____

   c. _____

   d. _____

2. The key to successful brainstorming is to maintain a _____ atmosphere so that all ideas are given value.

5

3. The round-robin method of guiding group discussions is used to ensure that _____ _____.

4. List three things you can do to build trust with other team members.

   a. _____

   b. _____

   c. _____

5. List three things you can do to get a team unstuck.

   a. _____

   b. _____

   c. _____

Chapter Six

Team Decision Making

Chapter Objectives

▶ Distinguish between *consensus* and *compromise*.

▶ Describe the benefits of consensus decision making.

▶ Identify consensus-building skills.

▶ Describe what to do when team consensus is lacking.

It had been a long morning for Bob, leader of the steering committee at a small-town Midwestern hospital. The committee had been talking for nearly 15 minutes and still couldn't reach agreement on whether to have the holiday dinner catered or have everyone bring a covered dish. Bob was getting frustrated because there were other, much more important items on the agenda that needed to be discussed. "Let's compromise," he suggested. "Let's have the caterer prepare and serve the main meal, but let's do the dessert ourselves. I'll even make some homemade ice cream. How about it?"

Thelma looked Bob in the eye and said, "You mean your wife will make homemade ice cream! You probably won't even lift a finger."

"You're right, Thelma," Bob retorted, "so instead I'll bake a cake while she makes the ice cream. Is that agreeable to you?"

"I might be able to live with that, if I can pick the caterer," Thelma answered.

"Go right ahead. You have my blessing," Bob said with relief. "Now let's move on to the next agenda item."

At another hospital, the seven-member leadership team was taking its first break of the day. They had spent the past two hours discussing a contractor's proposal for a new sewage treatment system. Although no votes had been taken, it appeared to the team leader that four people were in favor of the proposal, two were leaning in favor, and one was uncertain and perhaps even against the proposal.

The team leader suggested that the members look over the plans during the break and continue their discussions informally. They would reconvene in 12 minutes and continue the discussion. The team leader understood that this was the beginning of what could be a long day, because the final decision could only be made when there was complete consensus. That's the only acceptable way to make decisions in Kenya, Africa. If the team tried to compromise, they would be admitting defeat and their inability to work together.

Compromise vs. Consensus

Some people and some cultures won't settle for anything less than consensus when discussing an issue. They believe that having a unanimous verdict is the most important thing when reaching any type of decision. Others believe that there always has to be some give and take and that people have to be willing to compromise if anything is ever going to get done. Let's look at these two approaches from a team perspective.

Compromise

Merriam Webster's Collegiate Dictionary defines *compromise* as "to adjust or settle by mutual concessions." Compromise always involves some give and take. Unfortunately, some people wind up believing that they do all the giving and the other side does all the taking. Despite these shortcomings, compromise is still an accepted way of decision making. Most U.S. governing bodies, whether local, state, or federal, rely on the art of compromise. Generally speaking, the compromise process has served us well considering the hundreds of thousands of decisions these legislative bodies have made through the years.

To *compromise* means "to adjust or settle by mutual concessions."

You many find that there are times when members of your team have to compromise for one reason or another. Deciding to compromise shouldn't lead to a feeling of failure. In most cases, however, members will be more supportive of team decisions if there is consensus rather than compromise. We'll consider the consensus process in our next section.

6

Take a Moment

Think of compromises your team has made. How do you think members reacted to the final decision? What was your reaction to the compromises? Would consensus have been better?

_____

_____

_____

_____

Consensus is "the mutual feeling that all concerns have been addressed and that everyone has been heard and understood."

Consensus: Making a Lasting Decision

Consensus has been defined as "the mutual feeling that all concerns have been addressed and that everyone has been heard and understood."[2] Consensus does not necessarily mean always reaching 100 percent agreement. Some team members may not care for a particular decision, but they can still live with it and support it. They simply decide that any compromise or continuing disagreement with other team members would, in the long run, be counterproductive.

A decision made by consensus is one that team members believe in, and a decision that they can support in public. One of the major benefits of a consensus is that team members, who start off with differing points of view, eventually reach a common ground. After a well-managed and open discussion, differences that once appeared large are no longer seen as major obstacles.

[2] Steven Saint and James R. Lawson, *Rules for Reaching Consensus: A Modern Approach to Decision Making.* San Diego, CA: Pfeiffer and Co., 1994.

Consensus-Building Skills

Building consensus requires the effort of all team members, not just the team leader. All team members need to be aware of, and willing to practice, consensus-building skills. Here are six skill sets a team can use when it needs to reach a consensus and make a decision that everyone can support.

Skill Set	How It Works
1. Ask team members to write down their thoughts and feelings.	Be sure to have them consider both the pros and cons. Writing things down accomplishes two things: • It helps people crystallize their ideas. • When they start writing, they may find that their concerns aren't that significant.
2. Ask team members to state their position to the rest of the team.	Doing this in round-robin fashion gives everyone a chance to speak and be heard. It also ensures that everyone participates in the discussion, not just the vocal few.
3. Identify areas of agreement.	Use a flip chart or marker board and write down all the areas of agreement. Be sure that everyone participates. As the list is written, it will become obvious just how much agreement (or lack of agreement) already exists.
4. Identify areas of disagreement.	Follow the same procedure as above. Again, the size of the list can indicate just how much disagreement there is. Comparing the agreement and disagreement lists can give the team a good idea visually of where they stand on the issue. Once this list is developed, the discussion can be focused on addressing the areas of concern.

6

5. Resolve concerns.	Begin discussing areas of concern. In some cases, only a few members may have a given concern. Through the discussion, they may decide that their concerns aren't that significant and that they are satisfied that their concerns won't be a problem or they can live with them. At that point, cross the concerns off the list. Continue in the process until all concerns have been addressed and crossed off.
6. Identify the benefits and advantages of the decision.	Once all the concerns have been dealt with, it's important to get the team back on positive ground. Listing the benefits and advantages of the team's decision will help solidify the decision in members' minds. At the same time, they will be developing their own selling tool to use when they explain the decision to those outside the team.

Take a Moment

How often does your team practice these consensus-building skill sets? Rate the frequency of use from 1 to 5 according to the scale. Then identify which skills could be used more often and list some ideas for using them with your team.

	Rarely	Sometimes			Always
Ask team members to write down their thoughts and feelings.	1	2	3	4	5
Ask team members to state their position for the rest of the team.	1	2	3	4	5
Identify areas of agreement.	1	2	3	4	5

Continued on next page

Take a Moment *(continued)*

	Rarely	Sometimes	Always		
Identify areas of disagreement.	1	2	3	4	5
Resolve concerns.	1	2	3	4	5
Identify the benefits and advantages of the decision.	1	2	3	4	5

Which skills could be used more often? How?

_____

_____

_____

_____

6

When Team Consensus Is Lacking

No matter how hard a team tries, there may be times when it is unable to reach consensus, and some additional actions may be required. When consensus is the goal, every member has responsibility to take the lead in helping the team succeed. Regardless of whether you are in the team-facilitator role or are wearing your team-member hat, here are some specific actions to consider when team consensus is lacking.

1. **Contract for more time.**
    The first alternative is to ask for more time. For example, if a team decision is due by the end of the meeting, but it appears that it will be impossible to reach consensus, then the team should seek to extend its time to make the decision.

In some cases, the granting of extra time can be given by management or whomever the team reports to. In other cases, the team may have to make the decision for itself. Should it put off the decision or give itself more time? However, when making that decision, there's a catch—if the team is going to decide to give itself more time, it needs to be unanimous that it will do so. In other words, the team needs to reach consensus on the need for more time. If it can't reach consensus on more time, the actual decision needs to be reached using some other method.

> A nonbinding show of hands can be useful in gaining a sense of where the team stands on the decision.

2. **Take a straw poll.**
   A nonbinding show of hands can be useful in gaining a sense of where the team stands on the decision. If most members seem to be in favor, the straw poll may influence others to conclude that they should change their position. If very few members favor a decision, it may be best to withdraw the whole problem from the discussion and start again from another angle.

   An evenly divided straw poll indicates that a lot of work and convincing may be needed to reach a consensus. If so, the team will have to decide whether it's worth the time and effort that may be required to reach consensus.

3. **Hold small-group discussions.**
   If time is an issue, consider dividing the team into small groups for discussion. The small-group forum will give everyone an opportunity to share his or her views, which may not have been possible with the entire team. Those who might be reluctant to participate in the large-group environment may be more likely to speak their minds in the smaller group. When dividing into small groups, each one can be given the assignment to reach a consensus. Then when the full team is reassembled, each small group presents its position.

> One of the basic tenets of consensus is that everyone should have a chance to speak.

4. **Limit discussion.**
   One of the basic tenets of consensus is that everyone should have a chance to speak. Sometimes, however, you will have team members who dominate the discussion or those who repeat themselves just to be speaking. Limiting discussion

can help teams avoid having members who dominate or repeat themselves. Some techniques to use to limit discussion are to:

◆ Set a time limit on how long one person can talk.

◆ Have a rule that each person must be given the opportunity to speak before any one person speaks a second time.

◆ Talk to the offending persons in private and ask them to reduce their involvement.

◆ Use peer pressure in the team environment to squelch the overtalkative person.

5. **Verify assumptions.**
Perhaps the reason the team can't reach a consensus is that it is working from a faulty set of assumptions. For example, a team working on a flexible scheduling issue may conclude that it is something that everyone would have to accept if their proposal is adopted. Some additional discussion might reveal that the proposal is voluntary—not mandatory. In this case, reopening the discussion on some of the basic assumptions can redirect the team efforts and make reaching a consensus easier.

6

Take a Moment

Consider the last time your team tried to reach a consensus, but consensus was lacking. Which technique(s) could have been helpful in breaking the logjam?

_____ Contract for more time.

_____ Take a straw poll.

_____ Have small-group discussion.

_____ Limit discussion.

_____ Verify assumptions.

Why do you think the technique(s) would have helped?

_____

_____

Are there any logjams at the moment that could be broken by using one or more of these techniques? If so, what is the situation, and which technique(s) will you recommend to the team?

Situation   Technique(s)

_____   _____

                              _____

                              _____

Chapter Summary

Team decision making that relies on consensus is preferable to decisions that are the result of compromise. The skill sets described in this chapter provide specific ways to move a team toward consensus. When consensus is lacking, teams have options, such as contracting for more time, using straw polls, trying small-group discussions, limiting discussion, and verifying assumptions to achieve consensus.

Self-Check: Chapter 6 Review

Complete each of the following statements. Check your answers on page 116.

1. *Compromise* can be defined as a way of making a decision that _____

2. *Consensus* can be defined as the mutual feeling that all _____ have been addressed and that everyone has been _____ and _____.

3. When trying to build consensus, what are the two benefits of having people write down their ideas?

   a. _____

   b. _____

4. Why is it important to make a list of areas of agreement and disagreement?

   _____

   _____

5. If consensus is lacking and you want to gauge where people stand on an issue, what technique could you use?

   _____

6. What's one advantage of using small-group discussions to help reach consensus?

   _____

   _____

7. Why is it important to verify assumptions?

   _____

   _____

6

Chapter *Seven*

Wrapping It Up

Chapter Objectives

▶   List the options a team has after its goals are met.

▶   Describe the process to follow when disbanding a team.

"**S**o what else do we need to do?" asked Cheryl.

"Once we get the final report printed out, we'll need to present it to the management team on Wednesday morning," Ken replied. "After that, our task force is history."

"Well, we've had a good run," Cheryl observed, "and I think they'll be open to our recommendations."

"I agree," said Ken. "So, why the long face?"

"It's just that I, well, I . . . I'm going to miss those team meetings with Brian, Sandy, Susan, Dave, and you. We worked hard, but we had a lot of good times as well."

"I guess I'll probably miss them too," said Ken. "But I wouldn't worry too much if I were you. I heard there's another project coming up, and the company wants to set up a team to manage it. I've heard your name mentioned a couple of times . . ."

It's been said that all good things must come to an end—and that's usually the case with teams. As you have learned, most teams are formed to achieve a specific mission or set of performance goals. Once the goals are met, a decision has to be made regarding what to do with the team and its members. Let's look at the possibilities.

Determining a Team's Options

Most teams, such as those working on special projects or teams formed to plan a special event, are supposed to end. But ending doesn't have to be inevitable. There are three options available to teams who have met their goals.

1. **Extend the team's charter.**
   Many teams are formed for the purpose of coming up with specific recommendations. Once they develop their recommendations and get them approved, the plan is passed on to another team to implement the decisions. For example, a team may be formed to come up with recommendations for how to reorganize the company and a second team be given responsibility for carrying out the recommendations. Rather than changing teams at this point, however, some organizations have found it beneficial to extend a team's charter and give it responsibility for implementation as well. By extending the team's charter, management hopes to capitalize on members' sense of commitment to complete the implementation phase.

   A variation is to assign one or more members from the recommendation team, rather than the whole team, to the implementation team. This approach provides some continuity to the new team and ensures having members who have some knowledge about previous decisions. In some cases, management may appoint the same person to serve as leader of the new team.

2. **Recharter the same team.**
   When a team performs well, there is often a feeling that they should be given other assignments to tackle. When a team has achieved a great deal of synergy and been successful in accomplishing its mission, organizations want to take advantage of it. Consider, for example, an advertising team within an ad agency that comes up with a great ad campaign that brings a client lots of new customers. The client may go back to the ad agency and say that on the next campaign they want to have the same team.

> There are three options available to teams who have met their goals.

7

Keeping team members together for multiple assignments has some obvious advantages—members have established ground rules they can use again, they know their roles and responsibilities, members have learned how to work together and how to resolve conflicts. On the other hand, if the same team is given all the assignments, after a time they can become stale or less effective. Also, others who might be able to contribute are never given the opportunity. Each organization must weigh the advantages and disadvantages of rechartering when they need a new team.

3. **Disband the team.**
   Just end it! For some team members, that's their motto. They have accomplished what they set out to do and now they are ready to get back to business as usual. Disbanding a team is frequently the right choice. In some cases, the team has done all that was required. There is no secondary task to be assigned, and there is no new project on the immediate horizon. Team members normally go back to doing what they were doing before the team was formed, or they go to new individual assignments.

   While the decision to disband may be relatively obvious and easy, the disbanding process needs to be handled in a positive way so that team members and the organization have a sense of closure.

Take a Moment
What's Next for Your Team?
Think about your current team. Which of the alternatives just discussed makes most sense for it and why?

_____

_____

_____

Disbanding the Team

Once the decision has been made to disband the team, you can make the process run smoothly by following these simple steps:

1. Inform team members.

2. Evaluate the team's accomplishments.

3. Report the team's results.

4. Celebrate the team's success.

Informing Team Members

Informing team members may seem like an obvious first step, but that may be why it's often overlooked. In some situations, team members know it's time to end because they have accomplished their mission or their charter has run out. However, if other teams within the organization sometimes have their charters extended or are rechartered, team members may be wondering if that could happen to them. They need and want someone to tell them that they have done what is required and that they will be disbanded on a certain date or after they complete a specific task.

Although this may have been explained to members when the team was formed, it's also a good idea to do it again near the end as the team is winding up its work. Team members will appreciate the feedback, and it will help give them a sense of accomplishment. The announcement can be made by the current team leader or a member of management.

> If other teams within the organization sometimes have their charters extended or are rechartered, team members may be wondering if that could happen to them.

7

Evaluating Accomplishments

Everyone likes feedback—especially if it's positive. We want to know how we did in the eyes of others. If the team is being disbanded because it achieved its mission and performance goals, time should be set aside to evaluate the team's accomplishments. A review and comparison of the original objectives with the actual results can help team members have a feeling of achievement.

The team leader should take time to go over the results—both good and bad. This is a good time to review missed opportunities and discuss what could have been done differently. This type of review can be especially helpful for those who will be working on other teams in the future.

The evaluation of achievement can often be done hand in hand when the team is preparing its final report—the next step in preparing to disband.

Reporting Results

Normally, a final presentation must be made either in writing, or in person, or both. The presentation will be given to whomever requested the team to be formed and gave them their original assignment. The final report shouldn't be taken lightly, as it is a reflection of the team's hard work. Don't gloss over accomplishments or shortchange the team's efforts and the contributions of its members. Some of the things to consider for a final report are:

Normally, a final presentation must be made either in writing, or in person, or both.

◆ Team mission and performance goals

◆ List of team members and their backgrounds

◆ Summary of key accomplishments

◆ Research or data collected

◆ Obstacles encountered and how they were overcome

◆ Conclusions reached

◆ Recommendations

The team's final report should be presented in a professional manner to reflect the importance of the team's work. Some things to consider are:

◆ Put the written report in a binder or presentation folder.

◆ Prepare copies for each person who will hear the final report.

◆ Have several team members, not just the team leader, present the report.

- Invite those who will be affected by the report—management, stakeholders, and possibly even customers, depending on the nature of the report.

- Prepare visuals to support the presentation—color slides, overhead transparencies, or multimedia presentations can be effective. However, be cautious about using too much "sizzle" if there isn't any steak in your report.

- Provide refreshments to those in attendance.

- Decorate the presentation room with symbols of what the team has accomplished.

- Provide recognition to team members.

The specific things you decide to do will depend on your audience, your message, and the comfort of the team members making the presentation.

Celebrating Success

Everyone likes a party—especially people who have worked hard together. So don't disband the team without one final get-together—and one that doesn't involve work. Make it a true celebration. Some cake and ice cream might be good for starters, or whatever would be most fitting for your team.

A celebration should also include recognition of team members and their accomplishments—some teams have used items such as T-shirts, ball caps, pens, lapel pins, plaques, paperweights, and books. Use whatever it takes to let people know you appreciate their dedication and performance. Some teams also present "special" awards, in good taste, to team members who dealt with unique problems and resolved them or to those who were always late for team meetings or who missed assignments. The objective is not to make fun of shortcomings, but to recognize that they do happen and can contribute to team rapport.

Don't rain on the parade. You want people to really kick back and relax on that final celebration, so don't combine it with a final team meeting. Make it a separate special event. And, if possible, get someone else to do all the preparation and clean up for the party—and to pick up the tab.

> **A celebration should also include recognition of team members and their accomplishments.**

7

Take a Moment

Congratulations! Your team has accomplished quite a bit. Now it's time to formally disband. Use the space below to begin to formulate your plans for wrapping it up.

How will you inform team members?

_____

_____

How will you evaluate your team's achievements?

_____

_____

What will your final report be like?

_____

_____

How will you celebrate the team's success?

_____

_____

Chapter Summary

After a team has met it goals, its charter can be extended, it can be rechartered, or it can be disbanded. If the decision is made to disband, it is important to inform team members, evaluate success, report results, and celebrate success.

Self-Check: Chapter 7 Review

Complete each of the following statements. Check your answers on page 117.

1. List the three options teams have after they meet their goals.

    a. _____

    b. _____

    c. _____

2. List two advantages of assigning an existing team a new project.

    a. _____

    b. _____

3. Evaluating team success is important, because everyone needs some _____ on how they did.

4. Why should the team's final report be prepared and presented in a formal manner?

    _____

    _____

5. Why is it important to celebrate success?

    _____

    _____

7

Chapter *Eight*
Handling Difficult Team Situations

Chapter Objectives

▶ Name six difficult team situations.

▶ Describe ways to handle these difficult team situations.

ven if you and your team are committed to working together, from time to time you may encounter problems. Here are six difficult team situations and recommended ways to handle them.

What If the Team Never Seems to Get Anything Done?

Teams are formed for a specific purpose and should develop a clear mission and set of performance goals. Teams meet to discuss and work on their mission and goals. Sometimes, however, members leave a meeting feeling like they have wasted their time and nothing was accomplished.

You Should . . .

Insist that all team meetings have an agenda.

Insist that all team meetings have an agenda. The agenda should list topics of discussion and time limits for each topic. Other typical agenda items include a review of the team mission and performance goals, announcements, progress reports from team members, problem solving, and planning for the future.

The team member leading the meeting also has to be able to moderate discussion, get people involved, lead the team in making decisions, and manage meeting time. Someone needs to be assigned to record and distribute minutes of team meetings.

Members can then use the minutes to review what happened rather than taking valuable time at the next meeting reviewing old news.

Refer to Chapter 3 for more details.

What If There Is Chronic Conflict Between Individuals?

Some conflict is to be expected and, in some cases, even welcomed. If everyone on the team agreed with each other all the time, there wouldn't be a need for a team discussion—one person could make all the decisions. Ongoing and unresolved team conflict, however, can create feelings of uneasiness among team members and slow, or even stop, team progress. When this happens, something must be done.

You Should . . .

Verify that the conflict has no benefits for the team. If it does not, then use the four-step conflict resolution process:

1. Acknowledge the conflict.

2. Discuss the conflict.

3. Agree on a solution.

4. Monitor results.

In order to resolve a conflict, team members must agree that there is a conflict. Usually, a conflict will be obvious, but sometimes it may not surface because some team members won't be open and honest. The team leader has to make sure team members follow their own ground rules and that no one is holding back.

Once the conflict is acknowledged, more discussion is required to get a feeling of where the team stands on the issue. The discussion should be guided so that everyone gets a chance to speak and equal time is given to all points of view. Team members should focus on the conflict and not individual personalities. An effective discussion should begin to generate ideas on how to resolve the conflict.

8

> In order to resolve a conflict, team members must agree that there is a conflict.

The team must then agree on a solution it wants to implement. Then the results of implementing their solution must be monitored. Did the solution resolve the conflict? If not, what else needs to be done to resolve it? Or should the team try another solution. Resolving conflict can be time consuming, but if done properly, it can have beneficial results for the team.

Refer to Chapter 5 for more details.

What If One Person Is Too Aggressive and Dominates the Team?

Enthusiasm for the team and its goals are desirable characteristics. However, some members go overboard, become aggressive, and try to dominate the team. This behavior, if left unchecked, can have a negative impact on other members and ultimately on team performance.

You Should . . .

Focus on the positive team-member roles that are desirable and try to eliminate the negative roles. If you are the team leader, you can redirect the discussion by calling on other team members. You can also avoid eye contact with the person who is trying to dominate. If necessary, you may have to politely interrupt the person and indicate that you want the input of others.

Often, the aggressive team member will respond to a one-on-one discussion.

Often, the aggressive team member will respond to a one-on-one discussion. Assign a team member to talk to the person in private and explain how his or her behavior is being disruptive to the team. Using this form of peer pressure will often resolve the problem. If the problem persists, it may be necessary to remove the person from the team. This should always be a last resort, but it is something that may need to be done in the interest of team camaraderie.

Refer to Chapter 2 for more details.

What If the Team Never Seems to Be Able to Reach Agreement?

Some teams have difficulty reaching agreement—and some can't even reach agreement on how to reach agreement. They can't decide whether to go for consensus or compromise, or just to vote on every decision. The result can be chaos, confusion, and a lack of real progress in achieving the team's mission and performance goals.

You Should . . .

Take steps to build trust among team members. One reason for the disagreements may be that individual members don't trust each other. Trust can make conflict work if differences are brought to the surface, discussed, and resolved. Team members should be reminded of the importance of doing what it takes to build trust—team members must control their tongues, be honest, keep their word, act from facts, practice the golden rule, and support the team in public.

> **Trust can make conflict work if differences are brought to the surface, discussed, and resolved.**

Secondly, when team members can't reach agreement, evaluate your decision-making process—do you want to compromise or reach a consensus? If you want a consensus decision, use the following techniques:

1. Ask team members to write down their thoughts and feelings.

2. Ask team members to state their position for the rest of the team.

3. Identify areas of agreement and disagreement.

4. Resolve concerns.

5. Identify the benefits and advantages of the decision.

Using a systematic process for decision making can become the basis for resolving future disagreements.

Refer to Chapters 4 and 5 for more details.

8

What If a Team Member Is Not Pulling His or Her Weight?

On effective teams the whole is greater than the sum of its parts—as long as all team members do their fair share. Team members who don't pull their own weight can have a negative impact on everyone else. Uneven work loads can cause even the most enthusiastic member to stop and wonder if her extra effort is worth it when she sees another member not doing his part.

You Should . . .

Verify that the team member who is not pulling his or her weight is aware of the perception of other team members.

Verify that the team member who is not pulling his or her weight is aware of the perception of other team members. Perhaps the person is not aware of the problem and just needs some feedback to get going. Or perhaps there are extenuating circumstances that are getting in the way of performance. So before you take any action, find out why the team member seems to be giving less than is expected. Once you know the cause, you can deal with it.

Depending on what you find out, here are some things you could do:

1. Make sure that the team member understands and is committed to the team's mission and performance goals.

2. Be sure that the team member understands what's expected of team members.

3. Verify that the person wants to be a member of the team. On effective teams, the members hold each other accountable. When this mutual accountability is present, most team members will do what is expected of them by the rest of the team.

Refer to Chapters 1 and 2 for more details.

What If Some Members Never Seem to Follow Team Ground Rules?

Team ground rules are established so that all members know what is expected of them. Team members who don't follow the ground rules may have forgotten the rules, may not have understood the rules, or for some reason are just willfully ignoring them. Whatever the reason, their actions and attitude can soon rub off on others and negatively impact the team.

You Should . . .

Establish a process for dealing with broken ground rules. A team member who occasionally breaks a ground rule won't ruin the team, even though it can be annoying. Proactive teams decide ahead of time what the consequences will be for breaking ground rules. Among the possible consequences are:

| **Establish a process for dealing with broken ground rules.** |

◆ Not being allowed to participate in the rest of a discussion.

◆ Being given a less desirable task to complete.

◆ Being asked to take a leave of absence from the team.

Some teams take a lighter approach and hand out fines (a quarter or a dollar) to team members whenever they violate ground rules.

Positive, rather than negative, consequences usually work best. Take a proactive approach. When the team is first getting started, give positive feedback to team members who adhere to the team's ground rules and make positive contributions. Rewarding the behavior you want is a lot more fun for everyone than dishing out negative consequences when something isn't going well.

Refer to Chapters 2 and 3 for more details.

8

Chapter Summary

Even the best teams encounter difficult situations from time to time. This chapter presented six situations and recommended ways to handle them, based on the guidelines presented in this book.

Self-Check: Chapter 8 Review

Indicate whether the statements below are True or False. Check your answers on page 117.

1. True or false?
   One way to increase the likelihood of getting something accomplished at a team meeting is to have a written agenda.

2. True or false?
   It is best to ignore team members who don't follow the team ground rules because they will probably change their behavior on their own.

3. True or false?
   Team members who insist on dominating discussions and doing their own thing may have to be removed from the team.

4. True or false?
   It is usually easier to deal with problems after they occur rather than establishing too many rules ahead of time.

5. True or false?
   Some conflict among team members is to be expected and even welcomed.

8

Answers to Chapter Reviews

Chapter 1 (page 22)

1. A team is a small number of people with complementary skills who are committed to a common purpose, performance goals, and approach for which they hold themselves mutually accountable.

2. Any of the following:
   a. Accomplish more with less waste of time and materials
   b. Produce higher-quality work
   c. Are happier in their jobs
   d. Get the opportunity for personal development
   e. Are more flexible in how they approach problems
   f. Make customers more satisfied

3. Performance

4. Team performance should focus on results that balance the needs of customers, employees, and stakeholders.

5. Any of the following:
   a. The team lacks a shared purpose or focus.
   b. Team members are not committed.
   c. The team lacks support and/or resources.
   d. Team members fail to resolve interpersonal conflicts of team members.

Chapter 2 (page 35)

1. Expertise, impact, commitment, interpersonal skills

2. Potential

3. Interpersonal skills

4. Facilitator   (c)
   Troubleshooter   (a)
   Investigator   (e)
   Smoother   (d)
   Encourager   (b)

5. Dominator   (d)
   Arguer   (c)
   Nonparticipator   (e)
   Inquisitor   (b)
   Naysayer   (a)

Chapter 3 (page 53)

1. Proactive

2. Mission, performance goals

3. Name

4. a. Review team mission or performance goals
   b. Announcements
   c. Progress reports from team members
   d. Issues, problems, and solutions
   e. Planning for the future

5. Start, stop

6. One week

7. a. Create common expectations.
   b. Encourage desired behavior.
   c. Help a team self-manage itself.

Chapter 4 (page 65)

1. Things easy

2. Big picture

3. Focus on mission (c)
   Develop mutual accountability (a)
   Work alongside team members (d)
   Team-oriented attitude (b)

4. Environment

5. Expectations

6. Proactive

115

Chapter 5 (page 87)

1. a. Open—cannot be answered with a yes, no, or brief response.
   b. Direct—asked of a specific member.
   c. Reverse—question turned back to the person who asked it.
   d. Referral—Members of the team are asked to answer a team member's question.

2. Nonjudgmental

3. Everyone participates

4. Any three of the following: controls tongue; is honest with others; keeps his or her word; acts from facts, rather than opinions; practices the golden rule; supports the team in public.

5. Any three of the following: revisit the basics; go for small wins; try new approaches; bring in outsiders; change team members or team leaders.

Chapter 6 (page 97)

1. Requires each side to make some concessions.

2. Concerns, heard, understood

3. a. It helps people crystallize their ideas.
   b. When they start writing, they may find that their concerns aren't that significant.

4. Some team members can see visually how much agreement and disagreement exists on the issue.

5. Straw poll

6. Any of the following: saves time; shy persons speak up; everyone has a chance to speak; may reach consensus sooner.

7. To make sure that that everyone understands the issue and everyone is "reading from the same page."

Chapter 7 (page 105)

1. a. Extend the team's charter
   b. Recharter the same team
   c. Disband the team

2. Any of the following: have established ground rules; members know each other; members know their roles and responsibilities; members know how to work together; members know how to resolve conflicts.

3. Feedback

4. It's a reflection of the team and its work.

5. To let team members know their results and efforts are appreciated.

Chapter 8 (page 113)

1. True

2. False

3. True

4. False

5. True

Additional Resources

◆ Fisher, Kimball. *Leading Self-Directed Work Teams: A Guide to Developing New Team Leadership Skills.* New York, NY: McGraw-Hill, Inc., 1993.

◆ Katzenbach, Jon R. and Douglas K. Smith. *The Wisdom of Teams: Creating High-Performance Organizations.* New York, NY: Harper Business, 1994.

◆ Lloyd, Sam R. *Leading Teams: The Skills for Success.* West Des Moines, IA: American Media Publishing, 1996.

◆ Meeker, Larry, Steve Fischer, and Beth Michalak. *High-Performance Teamwork.* Amherst, MA: HRD Press, 1994.

◆ Parker, Glenn M. *Team Players and Teamwork.* San Francisco, CA: Jossey-Bass Publishers, 1996.

◆ Pokras, Sandy. *Rapid Team Deployment.* Los Altos, CA: Crisp Publications, Inc., 1995.

◆ Saint, Steven and James R. Lawson. *Rules for Reaching Consensus: A Modern Approach to Decision Making.* San Diego, CA: Pfeiffer & Company, 1994.

◆ Shonk, James H. *Team-Based Organizations: Developing a Successful Team Environment.* Burr Ridge, IL: Irwin Professional Publishing, 1997.